ADVANCE PRAISE

"Tyler has done an incredible job of diving into many leaders' biggest challenges to maximize their impact and influence, and provides a prescription for overcoming them. Through real, authentic stories and tactical applications, Tyler shares how anyone can step into their true leadership potential and break free of patterns we don't even know are holding us back. If you're ready to lead and live up to your God-given potential, this is the book for you."

—Jake Thompson, author, keynote speaker, and leadership performance coach

"I respect Tyler because he leads the same way he lives: with honesty, curiosity, and a deep desire to help people grow."

—Will Guidara, *New York Times* best-selling author of *Unreasonable Hospitality*

"In *The Things We Hide*, Tyler Dickerhoof gives leaders a powerful blueprint for elevating their inner game. With honesty, clarity, and practical wisdom, he shows how confronting our insecurities is the key to raising our performance and sustaining our impact. This book will challenge you, equip you, and help you show up as the leader you're capable of being."

—Alan Stein Jr., author of *Raise Your Game,* *Sustain Your Game,* and *Next Play*

"Tyler has a gift for making the hard stuff feel human. *The Things We Hide* is honest, practical, and full of stories that remind us we're not alone in our insecurities. This book gives you language for what you've felt for years and a path to move forward with more clarity and compassion."

—Chris Schembra, *Wall Street Journal* best-selling author of *Gratitude Through Hard Times*

"*The Things We Hide* is one of the most honest and courageous books I've read on insecurity, identity, and the inner battles that quietly shape our leadership and our lives. Tyler Dickerhoof doesn't write from theory—he writes from scars, stories, and deep self-awareness. Page after page, he invites the reader to stop hiding, stop performing, and start healing. If you're ready to lead with greater clarity, emotional strength, and authenticity, this book will challenge you, confront you, and ultimately change you. This is essential reading for any leader who wants to break free from what's been holding them back and step fully into who they were created to be."

—Chris Robinson, *USA Today* best-selling author and executive vice president of Maxwell Leadership

"*The Things We Hide* is a courageous, compassionate guide for anyone who has ever felt like they were too much and not enough at the same time. Tyler doesn't just tell stories; he hands you tools to understand your insecurity, own it, and finally stop letting it run the show."

—Claude Silver, chief heart officer of VaynerX and author of *Be Yourself at Work*

"Some books inform you. Some books inspire you. And then there are rare books like *The Things We Hide*. Books that confront you. Tyler Dickerhoof doesn't write from theory; he writes from scars. With courage, humility, and spiritual honesty, he takes you inside the places most of us spend our lives avoiding. The fears we suppress, the insecurities we armor up with, the wounds we try to outrun. This is not surface-level growth talk. This is deep work. The kind that forces you to stop performing, stop pretending, and finally tell yourself the truth. Every page feels like an invitation to step out of hiding and into healing.

"What makes this book powerful is not just the vulnerability, it's the clarity. TD doesn't just expose what's broken; he shows you how to rebuild with intention, ownership, and wisdom. This book will challenge how you lead, how you love, how you handle pressure, and how you see yourself. If you're tired of carrying what no one sees; if you're successful on the outside but restless on the inside; if you're ready to grow without hiding anymore, this book is for you. *The Things We Hide* isn't just a read. It's a mirror. And for those willing to look into it, it may just change everything."

—Roy Hall Jr., speaker, cofounder, and
executive director of the Driven Foundation

"Tyler has done the hard work that most leaders try to avoid, turning insecurity into clarity, confidence, and compassion. I've seen his growth firsthand and have personally experienced the power of his principles, and this book is both his story and his road map for anyone ready to do the same."

—Josh Combs, president of E3 Construction,
Dallas, Texas

"Every leader who is serious about leading themself well needs to read this book! Insecurity can so easily sabotage the best leaders. Tyler gives you the courage to confront the things you hide by vulnerably modeling the way."

—Jennifer Catron, best-selling author and
speaker

"*The Things We Hide* is the kind of read that gently encourages you while also giving you a loving nudge to step up. [Tyler's] a master encourager and connector, and it shows in every story he tells—including moments where insecurities, dead ends, and divine setups all collide. If you're ready to walk into the next year with more confidence and clarity, get this book in your hands today."

—Katie Quesada, keynote speaker and
founder of Better Said Workshops.

"This book is raw in the best way—real stories, real pain, real breakthrough. Tyler has a gift for naming what so many of us feel but don't know how to articulate: the fear of being rejected, unseen, unworthy, or not valuable. Page after page, he invites you to trade hiding for healing and insecurity for freedom. You won't just read this book—you'll recognize yourself in it, and you'll come out stronger."

—Amberly Lago, *USA Today* best-selling
author, speaker, top 1 percent podcast
host, and coach

"Insecurity whispers, 'You're not enough.' God whispers, 'You're my idea.' In his new book, my friend Tyler Dickerhoof points us to a life where we can walk and lead with confident humility. You don't have to hide. You can be what you've been created to be—the real you."

—Jeff Henderson, author of *What to Do Next*
and *Know What You're For*

"*The Things We Hide* is one of those rare books that doesn't just give you language for your insecurity—it gives you permission to finally face it. Tyler writes with a level of honesty most people avoid, connecting childhood wounds, leadership behaviors, faith, and personal responsibility in a way that feels both confronting and hopeful. As you read this, you will see yourself, your leadership, and your blind spots more clearly. This book doesn't shame you for your walls—it shows you how they were built and how to tear them down with courage and grace."

—Graham Cochrane, *USA Today* best-selling
author of *Rebel* and *The Effortless Business*

"Tyler Dickerhoof has created an absolute masterpiece in *The Things We Hide*. His authenticity, practical wisdom, and commitment to living life by design make this book both deeply impactful and immediately actionable. Tyler is one of the most humble, inspiring, and thoughtful leaders I've ever known, and that character shines through on every page. A must-read for every leader."

—Jordan Montgomery, keynote speaker and
USA Today best-selling author of *The Art of
Encouragement*

"Most people don't struggle because they lack potential—they struggle because they're carrying stories they've never examined. *The Things We Hide* is a courageous invitation to confront the insecurities shaping our decisions and reclaim intentional living. Tyler's writing is honest, clarifying, hope inspiring, and deeply impactful."

—Rory Vaden, *New York Times* best-selling
author of *Take the Stairs* and *Wealthy and
Well-Known*

"Tyler is a talented and spiritually gifted speaker, communicator, and leader. His authenticity and vulnerability are rare among leaders today, yet refreshing and admirable. He asks true and direct questions that really bring out what's on the inside of you. His stories, while incredibly painful, are stories you will never forget and will impact you and the way you think for a lifetime. *The Things We Hide* is a must-read book that, when you do the work and exercises provided, will leave you feeling freer from your insecurities than ever before. We need more leaders like Tyler in our world. I am honored to know him and call him a true friend."

—Dana Gentry, Keller Williams Realty
franchise owner, author, and speaker

"What makes this book a necessary companion for any leader is its proximity to the struggle. Tyler doesn't write from a pedestal; he writes as a leader who has navigated the grit of farm life, the weight of profound personal loss, and the hard realization that his own intensity was often a wall pushing people away.

"This book is not about fixing yourself; it is about owning yourself. Reading it feels like being invited into a conversation most leaders avoid but desperately need. The kind that changes how you lead by changing how you see yourself. It is a rare, honest look at who we are becoming while we lead, helping us shift from a life of self-preservation to a legacy of significance."
—Nikki Barua, serial entrepreneur, speaker, author, and CEO of FlipWork

"Every leader battles insecurity, but most of us hide it behind walls that limit our effectiveness. In *The Things We Hide,* Tyler Dickerhoof shows you how to stop hiding, embrace authenticity, and lead from a place of genuine strength."
—Mark Cole, CEO of Maxwell Leadership

"*The Things We Hide* is a rare kind of book, one that doesn't just talk about insecurity, but exposes how it quietly shapes our identities, our leadership, and our relationships.

"This book doesn't offer quick fixes or surface-level confidence tactics. Instead, it invites readers into the deeper work of self-awareness, accountability, and authentic connection. It is thoughtful, grounded, and deeply human.

"Anyone who wants to lead better, relate more honestly, or understand themselves more fully will find something important in these pages."
—Dr. Abbie Maroño, behavioral scientist and author of *The Upper Hand*

"Tyler is an impactful voice to lots of top-level entrepreneurs and leaders. And he understands what it takes to not just build things that matter but build them in a way that lasts."
—Brad Lomenick, founder of BLINC
and author of *H3 Leadership* and *The Catalyst Leader*

"Tyler, your vulnerability, combined with such practical insight, creates a transformative experience for the reader. You've articulated insecurity in a way that feels both relatable and empowering."
—Tricia Sciortino, CEO of Belay Solutions
and author of *Rise Up & Lead Well*

THE THINGS WE HIDE

THE THINGS WE HIDE

A GUIDE TO IDENTIFYING HIDDEN BARRIERS AND LEADING WITH AUTHENTICITY

Tyler Dickerhoof

THE THINGS WE HIDE
A Guide to Identifying Hidden Barriers and Leading with Authenticity

Copyright © 2026 by Tyler Dickerhoof

Disclaimer: This book has been published for the purpose of providing the reader with general information on its subject matter. The author and the publisher believe the information to be accurate and authoritative at the time of publication. The book is sold with the understanding that neither the author nor the publisher is providing professional advice, and the reader should not rely upon this book as such. Every situation is different, and professional advice (whether psychological, legal, financial, tax, or otherwise) should only be obtained from a professional licensed in your jurisdiction who has knowledge of the specific facts and circumstances.

For privacy reasons, some names, locations, and dates may have been changed.

Scripture quotations taken from The Holy Bible, New International Version®, NIV®. Copyright © 1973, 1978, 1984, 2011 by Biblica, Inc. Used with permission of Zondervan. All rights reserved worldwide. www.zondervan.com

Cover Design by Jesse Pierpoint
Interior Layout and Design by Alice Briggs
Editorial Team: Karen Rowe, Ginny Glass, Jamie Smith, Tessa Carvalho

ISBNs:
E-book: 979-8-89165-406-8
Paperback: 979-8-89165-407-5
Hardcover: 979-8-89165-408-2

Published by:
Streamline Books
Kansas City, MO
streamlinebookspublishing.com

CONTENTS

FOREWORD

've spent my entire career teaching leaders, and if there's one thing I know for sure, it's this: Leadership starts on the inside. Before we ever lead others, we have to learn how to lead ourselves. And that means facing the parts of ourselves we'd rather· not face.

We all have what I call blind spots or growth areas. Tyler calls them "the things we hide." Either way, there they are, quietly shaping our decisions, influencing our relationships, and capping our impact long before anyone else sees what's happening.

That's why this book can change your life.

In *The 21 Irrefutable Laws of Leadership*, I teach the Law of the Lid, which says, "Your leadership ability determines your effectiveness." What Tyler shows here is that insecurity often becomes that lid—quietly, subtly, and often without us noticing.

You'll read about walls we build: walls of intensity, inactivity, insensitivity, and isolation. And if you're anything like me, you'll recognize one or two of them in your own life. Recognizing your wall doesn't make you weak. It makes you wise. That's why I've always said, "You cannot grow yourself if you do not know yourself."

This book helps you know yourself. And with that knowledge, everything changes. Your decisions become clearer. Your relationships become deeper. Your leadership becomes more effective.

But here's the part most leaders miss: Authenticity isn't a weakness. It's your greatest strength.

After spending my life watching leaders, I know this: The leaders people follow the longest and trust the deepest are the ones who stop hiding—from themselves and others—and start connecting. People don't want a leader who is perfect. People want a leader who is authentic.

Your vulnerability has the potential to be one of your greatest leadership strengths. It invites relationship. It encourages trust. It gives others permission to stop pretending and start growing.

I met Tyler and Kelley in 2018 when they joined my Maxwell Executive Circle. Since then, I've walked with them on several continents through the work of the John Maxwell Leadership Foundation. I've watched them grow, not because they had all the answers, but because they stayed willing and teachable.

Tyler writes in this book, "We have to do the work on our own, but we don't have to do it alone." That's leadership. That's growth. And that's exactly how this book will walk with you—coming alongside you like a friend who knows the journey because he has walked it himself.

Before you turn the page, give yourself permission to be honest as you read. Some chapters may challenge you. Some may hit too close to home. That's all right. Growth always begins with this type of valuable awareness.

If you'll walk through this book with intentionality, you'll come away more grounded, more authentic, and more equipped to influence others at a deeper level.

The journey starts now. Turn the page. Let the work begin.

Your friend,
John C. Maxwell

INTRODUCTION

I met the sheriff deputy's eyes, done answering his questions. He sat on the hood of his car; I stood a few feet away. For ten long minutes, he had asked me question after question, and my response was the same: "It was an accident." When he asked again, I told him what I thought.

With all the power, intensity, and dominance I could muster from my five-foot, seven-inch frame, bulked up to a measly 130 pounds, I forcefully and directly stated, "I'm done answering your questions."

I pointed to my left, then said, "I am going to go into that barn to milk those cows right now. They won't milk themselves. If you want to come with me, fine. If not, *we're done*!"

As the last syllable left my lips, I turned and walked the three or four steps to the barn, which housed my family's fifty cows. I pulled open the white storm door and stepped inside. The wall—my shield for the next twenty-five years—now stood between me and the deputy, who was still perched on the hood of his car, contemplating it all.

The accident occurred on a typical summer day on our family farm. It was early June, and the grass that grew in the fields was ready to be harvested into hay. This crop would be used for the remainder of the year to feed a portion of our herd of cows. One of my chores was to prepare all the equipment we would use to harvest and transport the hay. On this day, I was working on the wagons that would haul the hay bales, greasing pivot points, checking wheel bearings, and properly inflating the tires for our two wagons.

I needed the wagons inside the shop to do the maintenance. The shop sat on a leveled pad cut into a natural slope, and the gravel driveway approached from below with a slight bend. I was trying to back a wagon uphill and into that turn. It wasn't working, so I drove down the hill, turned around, and tried backing the wagon from the upper side of the slope.

From the driver's seat, I saw my younger brother, Joel, to my left. His blond hair caught the afternoon sun, his smile gleaming. Joel was playing thirty or forty feet away in the strip of lawn between our house and the driveway. I waved, looked ahead, shifted from reverse to drive, accelerated, and made the loop. As I was driving back to the shop landing, I glanced at the driveway I had just driven. In the middle, on the gravel, lay Joel—motionless. Instantly, I knew something was wrong. I threw the vehicle in park, ran as fast as I could to the house, told my mom there had been an accident, and called 911.

It was four in the afternoon, and I had been trying to get this job done before the evening milking, which we typically started daily around four thirty. On this particular day, my dad had been away with my other brother, Trent, and would be arriving at any moment. Moments are memories, and others are a blur. I remember my dad coming home at some point amid the chaos. As he and I embraced, I hugged him so hard with so much pain and hurt that I tore the back of his shirt. My brother had died, and it was an accident.

I was fourteen, and Joel was three.

The Walls We Build

The barn walls of that moment soon took on greater significance and a more physical presence within me. The walls would become the structure that would hide the *things*—fears, hurts, and insecurities—within me. I would rely on these walls. Leaning against them for safety and structure. I would retreat within their confines to block the outside world. The walls would become my safe place and also my prison.

I stood behind the walls because the pain of trauma, the fear of being unworthy, and the insecurity of not having value screamed on the outside. You have walls too. Things we hide and walls we construct to protect ourselves. These walls create a safe house, or barn, of actions and reactions. Most of us don't call them that. We call them standards, boundaries, urgency, professionalism, or just "how I'm wired." But the wall is there—built plank by plank from fears and insecurities we learned to hide: not being enough, not having value, being rejected, being seen as a fool.

Fearing you're not good enough, you put your head down and push to accomplish. Afraid of rejection, you choose to avoid any interaction that could lead someone else to confirm your deepest fears; you are an impostor. Mocking, ridiculing, or jesting about someone else to make yourself seem superior or create doubt within them. Or check out. Disappear. Irish exit. "He was just right here a moment ago . . ." Ghosting. Going full airplane mode. Playing hide-and-seek by yourself!

Relate to a few of those? I've done them all.

It's not the fact that you and I have fears and insecurities. It's that our fears and insecurities create a barrier between who we are and how others experience us. The problem is the effect our fears and insecurities have on our ability to impact and lead others and ourselves.

When those fears get loud, our walls take over:

- Intensity: push harder, move faster, overwhelm others to feel safe.
- Inactivity: wait, avoid, procrastinate—hoping the problem resolves itself.
- Insensitivity: numb out, dismiss emotions; "toughen up" becomes a shield.
- Isolation: disappear, withhold, go airplane mode—if I'm not seen, I can't be judged.

These responses make us feel protected in the moment, but disconnected over time. These walls are exhausting. We feel compelled to perform to feel valued or to survive. We are living multiple lives and personalities depending on the people we are around or the place we work; always flopping, switching, or stuck. This internal exhaustion drives us to hide, and the things we hide become heavy, like a month's worth of groceries in plastic bags we're trying to carry up two flights of stairs all at once.

Soon enough, these walls define how we lead ourselves and others. We struggle not due to lack of talent or ability in the classical sense, but it is usually because of these hidden barriers, these walls that hold us in and eventually collapse in on us through suffocating unspoken fears, unrealized insecurities, and protectionism.

The walls drive people away. They damage relationships. They confuse people who want to trust us. They limit our impact at home and at work. And here's the kicker: What we hide always shows up. People may not know *what* it is, but they sure know *when* and *how* it arrives.

Like Google Maps but for You

In the chapters, lines, and stories of this book, you will read about my journey. I've had to recognize my fears and insecurities and own how I show up to others. I've had to reframe my toxic mindset and beliefs.

This journey will help you identify the walls that you use and how they create barriers in relationships and limit your ability to connect with others. Identifying the walls will allow you to put windows in them. The walls will always exist because we are human. But our walls don't have to be impenetrable; they can let light (and others) in!

This will allow you to show up authentically for others. The real you everyone wants to see and experience, not the contrived or manufactured person the world has convinced you to be to survive. This will take practice, working at it daily; reframing the mindset you have developed and built up to harbor the toxic beliefs that keep your fears and insecurities in control of your life. Like a long road trip to a place you love, the miles require patience, but the destination is worth it; this work takes the same steady effort, but it's possible. Ultimately, your greatest growth won't come from being more—only from being more yourself.

Here are the steps to get to where we are going.

1. Our fears and insecurities speak to us; they tell us to hide things. We will learn to recognize the language and express ourselves authentically.
2. The way our fears and insecurities speak to us establishes hidden barriers, walls that shape how we show up personally and professionally, impacting each relationship.

3. Learn how to take ownership of what others already see, without shame or guilt.
4. Learn how to lead with authenticity—being open, honest, and transparent without oversharing or becoming a victim.
5. Learn to embrace practices that turn vulnerability into true, long-lasting strength.
6. Learn to program a new growth-based mindset by establishing beliefs that drive thoughts leading to actions ending in results.
7. Understand you have to do the work on your own, but you don't have to do it alone. We aren't built to go through this life alone, no matter what our fears and insecurities make us believe.

When we get to where we are going together, you will be empowered to keep driving and doing the work, but I encourage you to ask others to join you.

You'll see that this journey wasn't one I took and adopted directly from others. It's original inasmuch as baking cookies from a package is from scratch. Not every idea is mine, but I did the work to assemble them. I read the books, learned to lead myself and others, and faced the hard moments when my walls appeared and disrupted relationships. I stayed in rooms with teachers like John Maxwell and built a community, the Impact Driven Leader Roundtable, where I could share losses and lessons and refine what you are about to read. I am by no means a master, but I am practicing every day toward mastery. A guide doesn't need all the answers, just the next step. I will share the steps that changed me and have helped many others. You will walk out of this book with clarity, confidence, and tools you can use the same day.

You will read about the barriers I discovered that were imprisoning me. I will roll out the framework I have used to build awareness, take ownership, and foster emotional intelligence. Last, several tools will help you create healthier, more connected communities and cultures. They are honest, accessible, and applicable to any leader regardless of title, position, or tenure.

I won't treat you like a priest taking confession, nor would I encourage you to use this book in that way for others. It is not a substitute for real clinical therapy. Hate to burst a bubble: It's not a quick fix. It is easy to read, but it will take some real effort to apply. There won't be a bunch of jargon, high-level theory, or hard-to-comprehend concepts.

I'm not the hero here. You are—because you're reading this book, willing to do the work, and ready to recognize your fears and insecurities, own how they show up, and reframe toxic mindsets and beliefs. That puts you on the path to grow for yourself, for others, and with others to make an impact! This book doesn't ask you to be perfect, only to be present.

Before we start to uncover the hidden barriers that keep us hiding, I'm going to ask you to go there with me—to look inward. Think about the things you have been hiding. Not the candy bar you stole when you were five, but the pressures, frustrations, hurts, ugly thoughts, and emotional beatdowns you give yourself. Think about the beliefs you hold about who you are, especially the ones that someone else planted. I'll bring the headlamp, but you have to do the looking. Remember: You don't have to do this alone. I'm going with you.

As I share my moments, I want you to reflect on yours. Start to recognize the feelings you have. The burning inside of you. The increase in your heart rate. The flush your face is developing. Then, how you respond to others in those moments, these are the early signs that insecurity is shaping how others view you, without even your knowledge or understanding. They are a response to the things we hide, and the walls do us more harm than good.

PART 1

RECOGNIZING FEARS AND INSECURITIES

HOW MY WALLS TOOK SHAPE

My brother Joel's death capped a difficult season in my life. The accident happened three days after my freshman year of high school ended. A school year in which I fought to find my footing. I was a very small kid entering high school. In November, I needed a physical to play basketball. I was five three and weighed 110 pounds. By March, I had grown to five seven and gained twenty pounds. During those four months, I grew physically but suffered tremendously socially and emotionally.

I hadn't played organized basketball before that year, but during a physical education class, a coach spotted me playing and encouraged me to join the team because I had a good shot. Just as we were starting the season, I attended a leadership conference near my school with other students from my FFA chapter. Trying to fit in and mask my insecurities, I found myself in a hotel guest room with a few of my sisters' friends, streaming and plugging the toilets with toilet paper and spraying shaving cream everywhere. We had locked the main door to make sure no one entered while we were creating carnage.

It wasn't until we exited the adjoining door into the other room that we realized the front door was still deadbolted. When the occupants tried to enter their room, they couldn't, so maintenance staff was called to disassemble the lock and open the door. I was sent home in the first few hours of the conference. My punishment also included not being able to compete in any contests with our FFA chapter for an entire year.

A few weeks later, we had our first basketball game. Being short, small, and lacking ball-handling skills, I didn't see much playing time. The one game I did get to play, I hit a short jumper from the middle of the lane and celebrated as if we had just won the championship. We were losing 57 to 23, now 25! My coach took extreme exception to my celebrating. He chastised me in the locker room, making an example of me for being out of touch. Most definitely not the way for me to build confidence or fit in.

About a month later, after basketball practice, a teammate and I were waiting at the school for our older siblings to finish a theater performance. Both famished and without money, I thought, *Maybe my sister has some money in her backpack.* He and I found where the drama club members had left their belongings, and I found a dollar of hers. My teammate decided to go bigger. He rummaged through a few other things and found more money. We left the room and bought some snacks from the vending machine.

The next day at school, we were both called to the principal's office. A theft had been reported, and the janitor had identified us as people they had seen in the area. He and I were both suspended for three days for stealing. Because it was still basketball season, he and I could earn our way back onto the team by running laps around the court. Our punishment was one hundred laps around the court for each day, totaling three hundred laps, or the equivalent of just over fifteen miles. I made it back on the team and eventually scored one more point that season. My high school basketball career scoring record stands at three points!

The next domino to fall for me was my freshman English grade. Already in dire straits because of my suspension and the mandatory zeros, I was strongly opposed to busywork. One of the class requirements was to keep a daily journal. I deplored this. Even at fourteen, as a freshman in high school, I was working at least five hours a day and over twenty-five hours a week, whether or not I was playing basketball. My typical day started with a 6:00 a.m. wake-up. Out the door to feed the young stock on our farm. Back inside the house at seven to shower and get dressed. Leave our house at about seven thirty for school. Home from school about three thirty. Back outside for afternoon chores and milking until I left for basketball practice that ran from seven to nine. On days when I wasn't able to come home after school because of games, I would do chores when I got home, around seven thirty or eight, for about an hour. That was my life. There was no hanging out with friends. There was no time to be creative. Every day was essentially Groundhog Day, and after writing out what my day entailed once or twice, I was done. I got an F.

For the record: I was suspended, failed freshman English, and still graduated from an Ivy League school. What happens to you when you're young doesn't have to be the end; it wasn't for me.

There was one highlight of my freshman year of high school. Because of my year-long FFA suspension, one contest where I wasn't able to compete was Dairy Judging, a Career Development Event (CDE) where students evaluate and rank dairy cattle based on physical traits that indicate milk production and longevity, and then provide oral justifications for their decisions.

I had competed in 4-H for numerous years, placing well in contests, and was excited about competing at the FFA level. It so happens that the 4-H and FFA state contests are held simultaneously in Ohio. Students and competitors in each division assess the same animals in the same arena at the same time, under the supervision of the same official judges.

While suspended from the FFA, my parents allowed me to compete in the 4-H contest. I won as the high-scoring individual. The next year, I could enter the FFA, but not the 4-H contest, since I had already won it. I placed second, and our team won, advancing to nationals in the fall.

What I learned during this season is that, no matter how hard I tried to fit in and overcome feeling like I didn't have value, what I was doing wasn't working for me. What helped cover the hurt I was feeling was being intense. A few years ago, when trying to understand the moment intensity became the proverbial wall that separated me, I reached out to a coach who had worked with me before and after my brother's death. They shared with me that I was always a driven, high-energy kid—at times a handful—but pretty likable and happy-go-lucky. After Joel died, I was just intense. Most people understood, knowing what had happened with my brother, and merely tried to support me in whatever way they could.

In those relationships, in childhood and beyond, there is one absolute that people would recognize: my intense nature. It made relationships hard. People would ridicule me, further triggering my greatest fear of not having value. My disposition to go as hard as I could would burn people out. Sure, there were times when I was easygoing and fun, but once I felt pressured or needed to protect, up went the wall of intensity. When I was trying to prove myself, I would be intense. When I was trying to protect myself, I would become intense, especially when I felt cornered, challenged, or triggered. My intensity would also sometimes lead to procrastination. Rejection was another insult to my insecurities; I would choose inactivity. Although I knew full well what to do, I chose not to do it, which would lead to more rejection.

I've recognized a couple of other ways, depending on the circumstances, in which I would react when my insecurity was triggered. I would be insensitive, an extension of intensity. I would discount others' struggles, pains, or difficulties. I had dealt with hard stuff, and I wasn't giving any grace to what others were dealing with; empathy be damned.

If any of those options—being intense, insensitive, or inactive—worked, I would isolate. I never attended the homecoming dance during my high school years; I only went to prom my senior year. I stayed at home most, if not all, weekends during high school. I didn't have a high school best friend. I had acquaintances and friends scattered throughout the state and country, having competed in dairy-related activities such as Dairy Judging and Dairy Knowledge/Quiz Bowl, a contest similar to an academic challenge, but focused on cows and the dairy industry. I chalked it up to not having those close friends and having to work. On Saturdays and Sundays, from the time I was eight until I left home to attend college, I would wake up at 5:00 a.m. I didn't have a curfew—I could stay out as late as I wanted, but I had to be out the door by 5:00 a.m. I don't ever remember being out past 10:30 p.m. on my own accord.

A further knock to my self-confidence and self-worth was being good at something none of my classmates understood or cared about. I won state and national competitions in both Dairy Judging and Dairy Knowledge Bowl, yet I was one of the smallest, slowest, and most awkwardly intelligent kids in my school. If I couldn't prove my value by being me, I would be intense and try to prove how smart I was. It never did, nor does it ever, go very well for me.

I essentially learned to build a house, four walls of protection around my soul, my insecurities. A wall of intensity, another of inactivity, insensitivity, and ultimately isolation. More on that in chapter 2.

CHAPTER 1

FEELING REJECTED AND UNWORTHY

My name is Tyler, not *Ty*!" I told my mom emphatically as I ripped off the name tag and shoved it in her hand, storming past her to walk the hundred or so yards from the bus stop to our house.

I was five years old when I got my first taste of name-teasing. Looking back, it was nothing compared to the ridicule my last name would later bring, but at the time, it was the most painful experience I had ever known.

My name tag read "TY," but the handwriting made it look more like "TV." It didn't take long for the kids on the bus to notice. "TV, TV, hey TV!" they chanted. Their taunts made me furious, which led to even more ridicule and teasing.

My dad shared that at one time, he thought I would end up having the nickname Ty. Nope, one day on the school bus in kindergarten put an end to that. Since then, the only people to have ever called me Ty are a few extended family members, which probably started when I was much younger.

It's amazing how one or two instances can sear pain, shame, and hurt so deeply into our minds and hearts that they alter an entire life. I can't say I was teased more than other kids; I just know it hurt.

In elementary and middle school, I was always one of the smallest in my class. The "TV" nickname was just the beginning—soon they found more ammunition: my big ears, my last name, Dickerhoof, even the fact that I lived on a farm. It was like arming a regiment with an endless supply of cannons, and each taunt hit me like a cannonball through the chest.

When our class had a "dress up like a farmer" day, I simply wore my daily work clothes—the same Key bib overalls, rubber "gum" boots, and ball cap I put on every morning at 5:00 a.m. for farm chores. The boots were as clean as I could get them, but the stench of manure is really hard to remove, no matter how much you scrub or disinfect. The ridicule I faced on the bus that day broke my heart. I never dressed up for school again. In some fashion, this one instance has stayed with me for over forty years.

The irony isn't lost on me: Today's society glamorizes Western wear and the farming lifestyle. When I share my childhood experiences of being mocked, most can't comprehend it. Only those who grew up like I did understand, nodding in shared recognition of that pain, ridicule, and embarrassment. What's most astonishing? I grew up and went to school in a rural community where many of my classmates worked their own family farms. Still, any hint of differences became a target.

One thing that hasn't changed in the last forty years is the obsession with athletic prowess. Being athletic, tall, and strong usually shields kids from teasing—a built-in defense against ridicule. But when my son once expressed how much he hated being one of the tallest in his class, how he endured his own share of teasing and ridicule, I could only shake my head in disbelief. All those years I'd wished to be tall.

For me, being small and slow, a deadly combination, made my youth sports career painful. At recess, when everyone played football, I was either never picked or chosen last. This pattern was the case for as many years as I can remember, and it wasn't limited to the playground. The same fate followed me through middle school. Standing about five feet tall, under a hundred pounds, and being one of the slowest players on the team, I rarely saw playing time.

Most teasing—and being passed over for teams—didn't faze me until I changed schools between fifth and sixth grade. Before this move, I knew my hierarchical standing. I had friends who, like me, either lived on a farm or had grandparents who did. I had friends who were on my soccer and baseball teams, and I enjoyed spending time with them. I was finding value in competing in dairy-specific contests through 4-H. I had a community of belonging.

This equilibrium was turned on its head when my family moved. My parents had the opportunity to purchase their own farm rather than renting as they had for the previous seven years. Even though the distance wasn't far—eleven miles—the culture, community, and school were completely different. Still a rural agricultural community, we moved from the most populated dairy farming county in the state to one with very few dairy farms. The schools changed, and so did all my social networks. The soccer and baseball teammates were now competitors or a distant memory.

Middle school is hard for so many people. It's a time of significant coming-of-age, when being thrust into a new network, with everyone jockeying for position, can be hard for the most socially adept and physically talented. I was neither. And trying in every way to prove myself ate me alive. While I had some friends, I was never able to develop truly great friendships from middle school through high school years.

I maintained friendships in all my networks, but often found myself at home alone on the weekends or during breaks. I had friends across the country whom I had met through dairy competitions, but nobody nearby I could invite to a sleepover. Because of the amount of work required on my family's farm, even the option of spending time with friends was challenging. I was able to attend camps through 4-H and dairy organizations, but the typical kid activity of playing at the park on summer days was never something I could do.

When we moved, I gave up baseball, mostly because I really didn't enjoy being a backstop for pitches. However, I continued to play soccer because my athletic limitations didn't hinder my ability to be a valuable team member. Yet I never had the opportunity to play with classmates. So even this made it challenging to form deep, meaningful relationships.

This was truly the crux. I was often far from my friends, who were in different schools, parts of the state, or even in other parts of the country. Because we shared similar interests, values, and lifestyles, I always felt like I was trying to fit in when I wasn't around them. I tried so hard to find my place. Looking back, because I had friends in other areas, focusing solely on friends with whom I shared everyday life wasn't a priority, which further divided me from others.

When I didn't get invited to birthday parties, I felt rejected. When I didn't get the invite to spend the night with a group of boys in my class, I felt rejected. When I wasn't selected for a team at recess, I felt rejected. This led me to isolate myself. I only remember having two birthday parties in elementary school, at five and eight years old, because I didn't have friends to invite, or they lived so far away that it wasn't possible.

All of this created a deep-seated insecurity regarding being valued and appreciated. *My biggest insecurity is not having value.* My athletic abilities didn't come until my mid- to late twenties. While I was intelligent, I drove people away by trying to use my smarts to gain acceptance. The areas where I did have success as a kid gave me confidence, but those instances and their relationships were few and far between. The damage was done, leading to repeated feelings of rejection and reinforcing the belief that the value I did have was unworthy.

I love all major sports, and being a valuable part of a team is exhilarating, regardless of the sport or contest. Yet being constantly reminded of my athletic worthlessness carved a void in my soul that no amount of success elsewhere could fill. Instead of embracing the areas where I truly shone, I kept reaching for acceptance in spaces that only offered rejection time and again.

I spent years running and hiding from my insecurities, chasing validation in all the wrong places while ignoring my genuine strengths. Denial never erases our wounds; it only forces them deeper, where they grow more potent and destructive.

Denial Doesn't Make Insecurities Go Away

Looking back, middle school is when I yearned so hard to be accepted and valued. Since then, as I've tried to come to grips with my insecurity and how it shows up, I've learned we all have fears and insecurities; the work isn't to avoid or deny them, but to own them and notice where and when they surface. I believe it's an absolute human truth, regardless of racial, social, economic, or health status.

In 2 Corinthians 12:7–10, the apostle Paul refers to the thorn in his flesh.

> [O]r because of these surpassingly great revelations. Therefore, in order to keep me from becoming conceited, I was given a thorn in my flesh, a messenger of Satan, to torment me. Three times I pleaded with the Lord to take it away from me. But he said to me, "My grace is sufficient for you, for my power is made perfect in weakness." Therefore, I will boast all the more gladly about my weaknesses, so that Christ's power may rest on me. That is why, for Christ's sake, I delight in weaknesses, in insults, in hardships, in persecutions, in difficulties. For when I am weak, then I am strong.

The Old Testament writers and Stoic philosophers refer to this as well. Moses in the Book of Exodus: "Moses said to God, 'Who am I that I should go to Pharaoh?'" (Exodus 3:11). Epictetus wrote in *Discourses* 1: "If someone does not value you, it is because he does not know you. Be content to be thought foolish and stupid in regard to external things." Seneca wrote in *Letters to Lucilius*, 13.4: "We suffer more often in imagination than in reality." Marcus Aurelius in *Meditations*, 8.26: "You have been made by nature for the purpose of working with others. To be anxious or angry is to revolt against this."

Scanning Buddhist, Hindu, and Islamic works to keep our bases covered too: "From craving arises sorrow; from craving arises fear. For one who is freed from craving, there is no sorrow—whence fear?" (Dhammapada 216). "When a man lets go of all desires of the mind, and is content in the Self by the Self, then he is said to be steady in wisdom" (Bhagavad Gita 2.55).

"And We will surely test you with something of fear and hunger and a loss of wealth and lives and fruits, but give good tidings to the patient—Those who, when disaster strikes them, say, 'Indeed we belong to Allah, and indeed to Him we will return'" (Surah Al-Baqarah 2:155–156).

Unilaterally, insecurity is our shared human condition. It touches everyone—the beautiful, the athletic, the intelligent, the charismatic, even the seemingly confident. Yeah, *everyone*. No one has the market cornered on fear, and no one is immune. If you are breathing, you've met these shadows. We all have. We're in this together.

Recognizing your insecurities is the first step toward healing them. I've seen this transformation firsthand while leading "the Roundtable," my group coaching program. There is a reason the Roundtable isn't a solo venture—we grow stronger when we face our insecurities together.

I was personally transformed in roundtable discussions I had with my mentor, John Maxwell, and others. In those groups, I learned the power of layered learning. As one member of a group shares, experiences, and learns, others in the group get to do the same. This accelerates every part of growth. It was here that I learned my personal value was not to prove, but rather to empathize with others. It was about accepting who I was, recognizing my value, and working to bring out the best in others.

Watching others in these cohort-based groups, I recognized my own journey in their struggles. Like me, they battled their fears and insecurities. I saw people struggle to own how they showed up, wrestle with deep-rooted beliefs and patterns that kept fears and insecurities ingrained in their actions and words.

In the first session of each cohort, I guide participants through the same exercise I'm sharing with you now—identifying their biggest insecurity. On this particular day, for whatever reason, only one member, David, was able to join.[1] As a person of faith, I don't see this as mere chance anymore; what once might have seemed like an unfortunate circumstance now feels more like a perfect coincidence or divine orchestration.

After brief instructions and housekeeping on Zoom, I jumped straight in: "What is your biggest insecurity?" For twenty minutes, David and I went back and forth trying to pin down an answer. "Where do you feel most uncertain?" "When do you feel anxious?" "Where do you lack confidence?" We were getting nowhere; each question led to another dead end.

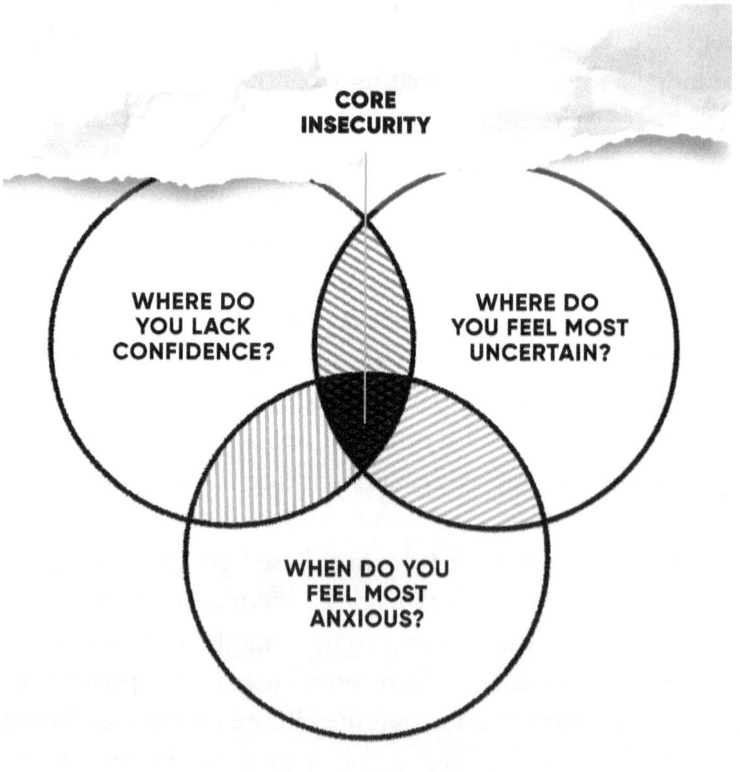

And then he was gone from the Zoom. I had hosted enough Zoom calls to know that losing someone during a call wasn't abnormal. But this was different.

I've known David for twenty-seven years; we went to college together, and his company has provided services to my businesses for years. He had attended my past Impact Driven Leader Summit. We've sat down in person and on the phone too many times in the last three decades to count on one hand, and he was gone. He exited the conversation faster than my first college girlfriend! (Our relationship lasted longer than twenty minutes, but not by much.)

I was just about to send David a text message when my phone buzzed, and it was him calling. "I can't do this," David blurted out as I answered the call. He was amped up and almost out of breath. "I can't be open and vulnerable when it's recorded. We can talk on the phone, but I can't share things when it's recorded."

In the five years I had led these sessions, this was the first time I had encountered this objection. I record the sessions primarily as a resource for attendees rather than for any other purpose. In the last couple of years, I have used a transcription service that not only records sessions but also summarizes them and emails each session to the attendees.

David shared that earlier in the session, as I was digging, discovering, and curiously probing to help him identify his fears and insecurities, every alarm was going off. "I can't do this. I can't be open and vulnerable." If a treasure hunter needed an X on the map, this is it.

I asked David why he struggled to be vulnerable and why he was concerned about being recorded. Quickly, he pointed to two relationships, one personal and one professional, in which his openness and vulnerability had been used against him. A double whammy of betrayal that had hardened into armor, making authenticity difficult both at home and at work. Rather than living a double life, he'd been forced to live alone on an island.

I am so grateful for the trust and relationship David and I have, and know wholeheartedly and without doubt the "solo session" was precisely what was needed. Had it been a typical group size of four or five, David would have flown under the radar, and it wouldn't have been possible to have had the same conversation. He would never have called me on the phone; he would have bounced and just said it wasn't going to work.

While recording sessions have been the default, I shared with David that it wasn't mandatory: My most significant focus was helping him discover and identify his fears and insecurities, own how they show up, and reframe his mindsets and beliefs. After one sixty-minute Roundtable session, David's life was forever changed.

If you know your fears and insecurities, you have power over them. If you don't know, they have control over you.

Admit That You Are Insecure

The most powerful exercise anyone can do is to admit that they are insecure. I have found that for myself and others, it's not only liberating but energizing. Being able to triangulate and articulate feelings of unworthiness—not being enough, powerlessness, lack of value, something being wrong with you, or rejection—finally allows us all to see how insecurity manifests in our everyday lives.

Before our session that day, David was blind to his insecurities. But seeing "this is being recorded" detonated something deep within him. His biggest insecurity—being seen as a fool—exploded like a claymore mine. His heart raced to 160 beats per minute, his face flushed, the hairs on the back of his neck rose, and his palms became sweaty as his fight-or-flight response kicked in. In that moment, his humanity—and his insecurities—were undeniable.

In the weeks that followed, David embarked on the same journey you'll take in these chapters. In the exercise below, you'll map your own triggers, name how they shape others' experience of you, and practice turning them into strengths—the first step toward authentic vulnerability that fuels real impact.

Exercise

As I mentioned, I found that working in groups was how I truly transformed and embraced authentic vulnerability. Although I had to start by doing the work on my own, I didn't have to do it alone.

Let's start there. What's your biggest insecurity? Use these questions to triangulate your response:

1. **Where do you feel most uncertain?**
   This can be where you face the fear of losing control, clarity, or stability. The answer could be "I feel most uncertain when I am put on the spot and have to come up with an answer quickly. Fearing that if I provide the wrong answer, I will be judged as not being worthy, capable, able, or qualified."

   Additional clarifying questions:

   A. What situations make you hesitate or question your decisions?
   B. When plans change unexpectedly, what concerns you the most?

C. If areas of your life feel "foggy" or unpredictable right now, in what way do they make you uneasy?

D. When you feel uncertain, what story do you tell yourself about what that means?

2. **Where do you lack confidence?**

A lack of confidence is associated with performance-based insecurity, a belief that worth must be earned and thereby judged by accomplishments. I faced this often when it came to sports. I had confidence when I competed where I was skilled and talented, but athletically, I struggled early in life. Professionally, this occurred when I felt overshadowed by someone else's performance, such as a better salesperson or a peer who had achieved more in life: accomplishments, awards, possessions, or net worth.

Where I have lacked confidence the most, I try to overcompensate and express what I have accomplished or what expertise I have. When I feel unvalued and discounted, I will try to show off my value. People who go above and beyond to display possessions, accolades, acquaintances, or status often do so to counter their lack of confidence. Others will become completely reserved, backing away and removing themselves from situations where they need to perform, thinking they can't lose if they don't play the game.

Additional clarifying questions:

A. In settings where you feel out of place, do you hold back your ideas or voice?

B. What fears arise before you take action or lead others?

C. When you succeed, do you fully receive it—or minimize it?
D. Do you often compare yourself to others, making excuses or justifying?
E. What repeated message do you hear in moments of doubt?

3. **When do you feel most anxious?**
Anxiety often reveals relational or belonging insecurity—fear of being rejected, exposed, or unseen. Much like David, I have felt most anxious when I feel I have to prove myself to gain acceptance. This anxiety drives me to push. David shuts down and backs away; others become cutting, attacking, or catty. When anxiety pops up, makes you feel flushed, or triggers the fight-or-flight response with no obvious signs of threat, these are our internal responses to fear.

Author Dr. Caroline Leaf shared with me during our podcast that our brain cannot discern between perceived or actual threats in regard to our response.[2] A threat is a threat, whether it's an insecurity of value or a mountain lion about to pounce on you!

Additional clarifying questions:

A. When does your body tighten or your heart race?
B. What outcomes or situations trigger the most worry for you?
C. Who are you most afraid of disappointing?
D. When anxiety rises, what are you trying to protect?

Triangulating Your Core Insecurity

Instructions
Look across your three sets of answers. What are the *recurring themes or emotions*? Common threads may include:

- Fear of rejection
- Fear of failure
- Fear of not being enough
- Fear of losing control
- Fear of not mattering

Core Insecurity Statement
Complete this sentence in your own words:
    "Deep down, I fear that ________________________________."

Looking Ahead

You've named the wound—rejection, inadequacy, unworthiness, a fear of not mattering. In chapter 2, we'll trace how that insecurity doesn't stay inside; it leaks into meetings, teams, families, and friendships, shaping how others experience you long before you notice it.

EFFECT ON THOSE AROUND YOU

The words landed hard: "This is how you deal with things." I lowered my head and let them sink in. I knew who said them, and though they were hard to hear, they comforted me. I was sitting on the bench inside the gym locker room, where I had just finished my workout. I had gotten dressed, filled my shaker cup with water and protein powder, and was just about to take a sip when I heard God speak to me. It was 2016, and the gym my wife, Kelley, and I owned was facing an employment challenge.

We started the gym, Training Ground, in 2013, after I left my career as a commodity consultant and dairy nutritionist. I had worked at the Cornell University Fitness Centers during college and had been working out fanatically for fifteen years. Kelley had taught fitness classes for a few years, and we thought, *Why not start a gym!* While we had some experience, we knew we didn't have enough to run a gym full-time—to teach classes, train clients, and market the business. We approached another couple about the opportunity and established a loose partnership agreement: We would provide funding and support, and they would operate the gym and handle marketing. That lasted about thirty days.

With no skin in the game and the hours proving more demanding than expected, they bowed out. In one weekend, we went from 25 percent involvement in the day-to-day operations to 100 percent. But we did what we do: put our heads down and get to work. This led to some success, numerous friendships, a positive impact, and employees who truly valued the environment we created. But true to its name, Training Ground was just that: a business, leadership, and life training ground.

We were learning a simple standard: Keep your word—show up when you say you will, and do what you said by when you said it. Just before Christmas, two of our trainers, fresh out of college, were learning the ropes while I was learning how to encourage, hold people accountable, and mentor effectively. On one particular day, I went to the gym to do the weekly cleaning. I drove up, and to my surprise, both of the trainers and their friends were there working out. Normally, I would welcome and encourage this; however, in this instance, one of the trainers had called off sick the day before, and I was there to do the cleaning they were supposed to have done.

I was upset. Not because they called off sick, not because I was doing their work, not because they were at the gym working out during closed hours. I was upset about *all* of it. The lack of understanding, communication, and ownership in a small business with fewer than five employees is that someone else has to do your job in addition to their own when you don't do yours.

I met with the trainer. I tried to express the expectations and where they had fallen short. This person was a valuable asset to the organization; they were young but had been part of the team for years and were a great individual who cared deeply for coworkers and clients. They were part of the gym, just like Kelley and me, and I thought they would soon be running the gym and potentially taking it to new heights. I wanted the best for them.

So in the middle of conflict, challenge, and difficulty, what did I do? I put my head down and pushed. I expressed my extreme displeasure with their actions and said I would not tolerate it. There was no place for taking advantage of me or anyone else. Ultimately, it was get with it or get gone.

Ten years later, I can clearly see what went wrong: The manifestation of my insecurities and intensity clashed with theirs.

Six months before this incident, we had brought on a partner. This person owned another gym in a different part of the city and brought much more training experience than we had. They offered the chance to expand our business and to provide the mentorship I wasn't able to offer our young trainer. However, the young trainer didn't see it that way. Instead, they felt threatened that this partner was essentially pushing them out. My intense reaction led to the young trainer leaving, primarily due to a misunderstanding and my own immaturity as a leader.

Responding with intensity is what I did to survive and to thrive. Intensity is funny like that. Molly Sloan, an inaugural member of the Impact Driven Leader Roundtable, described it in this way. Intensity is like a bright light; in the middle of the day, it's fine, but at 3:00 a.m., when your kids walk in the bedroom and turn on the lights, the reaction is the same: hands covering your eyes, blocking the light, and begging, "make it go away."

The Four Walls of Insecurity

The walls we construct limit our ability to connect with others. People know and recognize when our insecurities show up. They may not know what our insecurities are, but they know when they show up because of how we act and react. These walls establish a barrier and limit our ability to connect with others.

That moment in the locker room, I finally saw the wall for what it was: a relationship barrier, a symptom of the four defenses I'd forged years earlier, as I shared in the preface. Now, let's focus on the relational impact: what each wall looks like to others and how it lands on a team.

Intensity

Intensity is like a bulldozer, used for good: It clears a path or space for things to happen. Used destructively, it will leave carnage in its wake. These are burned-out and spoiled relationships where others feel used, taken advantage of, and pushed away. An intense person is often described as difficult. A hard charger who is all about themselves and what they want to accomplish: Their expectations are often imposed on others and are frequently unreasonable. Our business environments and many high-achieving organizations value intensity as a means to "get things done." There is no doubt that intensity can be used to achieve and accomplish. But the expense of their intensity is costly.

Inactivity

Inactivity is knowing what to do, but hoping the situation resolves itself without direct intervention or action. This is knowing what needs to be done but fearing doing it for any number of reasons, including potential rejection or feeling incapable, underqualified, or unable to do what needs to be done. I had this happen in discussions with clients, employees, and bosses. If I put my head in the sand and let things play out, maybe it would take care of itself. It was a way to save face and avoid doing the hard things. This is different from isolation, though they share a corner. Inaction is expecting something to occur on its own or someone else to handle a situation you don't want to deal with, so you don't have to act. Inaction is classic procrastination: the practice of doing nothing to protect ourselves from potential triggers of fear and insecurity.

Insensitivity

Insensitivity is the fullest extent of callousness. Others' thoughts, opinions, or feelings are irrelevant when it comes to protecting yourself from your fears and insecurities. Often, insensitivity is a form of compensation for being questioned for being too soft, empathetic, forgiving, or trusting. Get burned a couple of times and empathy goes out the window, replaced by insensitivity. Insensitivity can easily spill over to the corner it shares with intensity, and both walls are formidable. Be so intense and so insensitive that it seals away any potential vulnerability that can be used against you.

Many feel that insensitivity is needed to drive resilience and personal fortitude. The reality is that it causes people to disassociate, shut down, and feel unsafe. Choosing to be insensitive has been a leadership mechanism for many, instead of showing partiality and favoritism in the spirit of fairness. This wall created such a dilemma during the COVID-19 era and subsequent Great Resignation because organizations felt that if they chose to connect, understand, and accommodate their employees, they would be taken advantage of and lose the power dynamic. It simply drove good people away.

Isolation

Isolation is checking out. Like the Homer Simpson meme where he slides backward into the hedges to disappear, isolation is removing yourself rather than facing a situation. This can show up in many ways, including the leader who chooses not to "lead" meetings and be quiet because they don't want to prove their perceived inadequacy or incompetence, or a person who often removes themselves from meetings because they have nothing to add. People who put up the wall of isolation adhere to the motto, "Better to remain silent and be thought a fool than to speak and remove all doubt," as written by Maurice Switzer[3], which closely follows Scripture: "Even fools are thought wise if they keep silent, and discerning if they hold their tongues" (Proverbs 17:28).

In Patrick Lencioni's book *The Five Dysfunctions of a Team*, the character Martin Gilmore expressed this wall by making it clear to others that the meetings were beneath him. As Patrick writes,

> In fact, he rarely participated. It wasn't that he refused to attend those meetings (even Jeff wouldn't allow such a blatant act of revolt); it was just that he always had his laptop open, and he seemed to be constantly checking e-mail or doing something similarly engrossing. Only when someone made a factually incorrect statement could Martin be counted on to offer a comment, and usually a sarcastic one at that.
>
> At first, this was tolerable, maybe even amusing, to Martin's peers, who seemed in awe of his intellect. But it began to wear on the staff over time. And with the company's recent struggles, it had become an increasingly grating source of frustration for many of them.[4]

A final example: At a leadership conference, I saw a YouTuber with three million followers slip into the Starbucks line and try to hide—not to avoid a crowd but from the fear of being found out, of not measuring up, of being seen as an impostor—or worse, a fake!

For me, I would isolate myself in any social situation where I felt unqualified, undervalued, or unwelcome. I would stand in the corner and watch the crowd. In my opinion, an insecure introvert uses isolation as an excuse: "I'm an introvert, so I'll work by myself, be myself, only play individual sports, or refrain from team exercises due to fear and insecurity."

Insecurity Impact Assessment

I've created an assessment to help you quickly identify which wall or corner you lean against. To help better describe each wall, I have pulled together two examples from popular books. *The Five Dysfunctions of a Team* by Patrick Lencioni and *Dare to Lead* by Brené Brown.

Examples: (ChatGPT Created)

The Five Dysfunctions Characters Through the Lens of Insecurity

Patrick Lencioni's *The Five Dysfunctions of a Team* introduces us to a cast of leaders whose struggles mirror the insecurities many of us face. When viewed through the Insecurity Impact Framework (isolation, inactivity, insensitivity, intensity), their behaviors become even clearer.

Kathryn Petersen—CEO (The Antidote)

- **Story:** The new CEO who models humility, patience, and persistence. She builds trust and holds the team accountable.
- **Insecurity Fit:** *None*—she demonstrates the antidote: **healthy vulnerability**.

Jeff Shanley—Former CEO/Head of Business Development

- **Story:** Struggles to fully engage after stepping aside as CEO. At times, avoids tough conversations.
- **Insecurity Fit: Inactivity**—knowing what needs to be said or done, but shrinking back.

Mikey Bebe—Head of Marketing

- **Story:** Brilliant, but openly dismissive of the team process. Rolls her eyes in meetings, questions the value, refuses to commit. Eventually fired.
- **Insecurity Fit: Isolation + Insensitivity**—pulls away while dismissing others' contributions.

Martin Gilmore—Chief Technologist

- **Story:** The "scientist" type. Smart, analytical, but disconnected. Thinks meetings are a waste and prefers working alone.
- **Insecurity Fit: Isolation**—brilliant, but retreats from the team environment.

Jan Mersino—CFO

- **Story:** Cautious and skeptical. Initially guarded, hesitant to open up, but eventually leans into trust.
- **Insecurity Fit: Inactivity**—sits back rather than stepping forward.

Carlos Amador—Head of Customer Support

- **Story:** Passionate and outspoken. Sometimes too forceful, but his energy eventually gets channeled for good.
- **Insecurity Fit: Intensity**—strong personality that can bulldoze others if unchecked.

Summary Table

Character	Role	Insecurity Category	Lesson for Leaders
Kathryn Petersen	CEO (leader)	Antidote (healthy vulnerability)	Model authenticity and accountability
Jeff Shanley	Former CEO/Head of Business Development	Inactivity	Avoid retreat; speak up and act
Mikey Bebe	Head of Marketing	Isolation + Insensitivity	Presence matters as much as performance

Character	Role	Insecurity Category	Lesson for Leaders
Martin Gilmore	Chief Technologist	Isolation	Brilliance without connection limits impact
Jan Mersino	CFO	Inactivity	Courage to contribute builds trust
Carlos Amador	Head of Customer Support	Intensity	Passion needs balance with humility

Insecurity and Leadership Armor

(Inspired by Brené Brown's *Dare to Lead*)

Brené Brown describes how leaders "armor up" when insecurity drives their actions. That armor looks different depending on the person—but it always limits trust, connection, and growth. When we place it alongside the Insecurity Impact Framework, the overlap is clear.

1. Isolation—Armored Leadership: Hiding Behind Walls

- **Armor Behavior:** Withdrawing, cynicism, refusing to be vulnerable. Leaders think: *If I don't show up fully, I can't be hurt.*

- **Daring Alternative:** Choosing **connection and vulnerability**. Stepping into the room, speaking honestly, and letting others see your humanity.

2. Inactivity—Armored Leadership: Avoiding Hard Things

- **Armor Behavior:** Leaders delay or sidestep crucial conversations, hoping conflict or problems will just disappear.
- **Daring Alternative:** Practicing **courageous accountability**. Naming the issue, addressing it early, and modeling that clarity is kindness.

3. Insensitivity—Armored Leadership: Devaluing Emotions

- **Armor Behavior:** Believing feelings are a weakness. Saying things like "suck it up" or ignoring the human impact of decisions.
- **Daring Alternative: Empathy and curiosity.** Leaning in to listen, seeking to understand before being understood.

4. Intensity—Armored Leadership: Overcontrol and Perfectionism

- **Armor Behavior:** Bulldozing with force or micromanaging. Driving outcomes with fear, domination, or an obsession with being right.
- **Daring Alternative: Grounded confidence.** Leading with clarity and humility, creating space for others to contribute their best.

Summary Table

Insecurity Category	Armored Leadership (Brown)	Daring Leadership Alternative
Isolation	Withdrawing, cynicism, self-protection	Vulnerability & connection
Inactivity	Avoidance of conflict or accountability	Courageous accountability
Insensitivity	Dismissing emotions, "toughen up"	Empathy & curiosity
Intensity	Perfectionism, control, and bulldozing	Grounded confidence & humility

Follow this link to take the assessment or scan the QR code that follows:

https://www.tylerdickerhoof.com/insecurity

Insecurity Impact Assessment

Instructions:

- For each of the twelve questions, rate yourself on a scale of 1 to 5:
  - **1 = Never**
  - **2 = Rarely**
  - **3 = Sometimes**
  - **4 = Often**
  - **5 = Always**
- Add up the scores in each category (Isolation, Insensitivity, Inactivity, Intensity).
- Your highest score indicates your most common insecurity response.

Insecurity Impact Assessment (Twelve Questions)

Isolation

1. In group settings, how often do you find yourself withdrawing, sitting on the sidelines, or avoiding engagement?
2. When leading a team, do you hesitate to speak up or contribute because you fear your input won't matter?
3. How often do you connect easily with large audiences (online, professional) but struggle to engage in one-on-one or small group conversations?

Insensitivity

4. How often do you dismiss others' opinions or feelings because you believe they should "deal with it"?
5. When someone shares a personal struggle, do you tend to overlook it and focus only on tasks or results?
6. Do people ever describe you as unapproachable, blunt, or uninterested in how your actions affect others?

Inactivity

7. When faced with a difficult but necessary decision, how often do you delay or avoid taking action?
8. Do you find yourself waiting for problems to "work themselves out" rather than addressing them directly?
9. How often do you know the right next step but hold back because it feels uncomfortable or risky?

Intensity

10. Do people often tell you that your expectations or pace feel overwhelming or unreasonable?
11. How often do you drive forward with goals or standards even when it strains relationships?
12. Do you ever pride yourself on being a "hard charger," even if it means others see you as pushy or domineering?

Scoring Bands

Per Category (Max = 15 points, Min = 3 points):

- **12–15:** This insecurity response shows up *strongly* and likely impacts your relationships or leadership.

- **8–11:** This response shows up *sometimes* and may surface in specific situations.
- **3–7:** This response is *less common* for you, though it may still appear under stress.

Quadrant Descriptions

- **Isolation (bottom right):** You step back, withdraw, or choose silence—often from fear of not belonging or not being valued.
- **Inactivity (bottom left):** You stay put, avoid discomfort, and hope issues resolve themselves.
- **Insensitivity (top right):** You protect yourself by ignoring others' perspectives and emotions, prioritizing "toughness."
- **Intensity (top left):** You push harder, demand more, and bulldoze—believing results matter more than relationships.

Insecurity Impact Matrix

How to Use the Matrix

1. Add up your scores in each category.
2. Place yourself in the quadrant that has your **highest score**.
3. If two categories tie, you're likely shifting between those insecurity responses depending on context.

INSECURITY IMPACT MATRIX

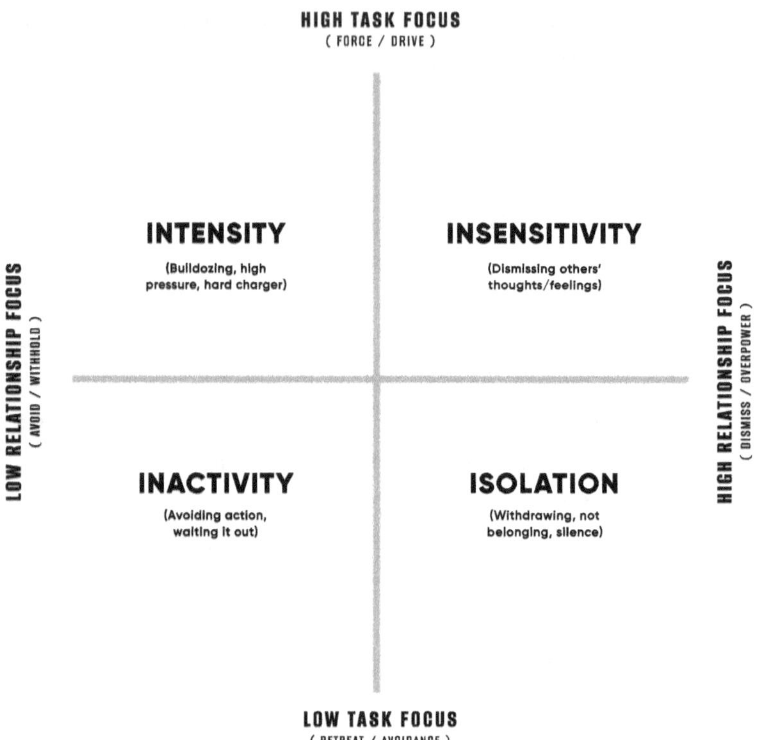

Interpretation Guide

- **Isolation (Withdrawing):** You may struggle with belonging, choosing to retreat rather than engage—even when your presence or voice is needed.
- **Insensitivity (Dismissing):** You may protect yourself by disregarding others' perspectives or emotions, focusing only on toughness or results.

- **Inactivity (Avoiding):** You may avoid discomfort by waiting for problems to resolve on their own, even when you know action is needed.
- **Intensity (Overpowering):** You may overcompensate with force, drive, or high expectations—sometimes bulldozing others in the process.

We've seen how your walls land on other people, sometimes like a spotlight, sometimes like a bulldozer. In chapter 3, we'll turn the lens inward to tally the personal cost: the fatigue, isolation, and missed connection those same walls create in you.

EFFECT ON YOU

I moved to California in the summer of 2001 to take my first postcollege job, a dairy management consultant for a large multinational organization. The term "dairy management consultant" (DMC) is a relatively broad way to describe how I got paid, being a dietitian for cows. Beyond the role as nutrition adviser, a DMC is essentially a trusted adviser who helps dairy operations run more efficiently, profitably, and sustainably—part nutritionist, part business strategist, part coach, and part systems optimizer. At times, the role even extends to a marriage or family counselor and a sales broker too.

I had decided to pursue a career in California for several reasons. In the early 2000s, California was experiencing massive growth within the dairy industry. Dairy farms were expanding nearly exponentially as they sold their land and operations just east of Los Angeles and relocated to the Central Valley. The farms would often quadruple their operations as part of the relocation process, primarily to mitigate tax liabilities. This drove growth in the number of cows in the state and in milk production.

With more cows and bigger farms, the need for more industry support also increased.

Next, going to school in upstate New York, I saw enough snow to last me a lifetime. Growing up in northeast Ohio, I was familiar with winter. But New York's snow is different. Away from the massive lake-effect bands that dump feet of snow on Buffalo and Watertown, cities just east of Lake Erie, the snowfall in other places was no joke. During my freshman year of college, I returned to Ithaca in mid-January. While driving to get my haircut with a buddy, I looked out the passenger window of the sedan; to my chagrin, the snowbank outside was at eye level. I had *never* experienced this, and, as most New Yorkers were quick to tell me, *this was nothing*. Quickly, the thought of sun and seventy degrees in January sounded a lot more inviting.

Last, I had a few fraternity brothers living and working in California—one in the north central part of the Central Valley, in Modesto, and the other in Bakersfield. The company I worked for had a central office in the same area as Modesto, so when I moved to California, I lived with my friend, who had arrived in California the previous year and was working on a dairy farm. As was customary for people in his position, the farm provided housing, and there was no issue with my being his roommate. It made the transition to a new state and a new career that much easier. His group of friends would soon become my social group, most of whom are still close friends to this day.

Relocation and Dislocation

Nine months into my job, my boss asked me to relocate to Bakersfield, in the southern part of the state. While I had mostly been in training, spending time with seasoned consultants on the West Coast, I had picked up a few clients, primarily through my social connections. Relocating three hours would move me to an entirely new area and a significantly different social group. I only knew one person who lived in Bakersfield, and I reached out to see if I could live with him. In early March of 2002, I moved everything I owned into a new house and a new city.

I would split my time between the two regions. In the Bakersfield area, I would canvas the local farms to establish new connections and relationships with them and other service providers. Every other week, I'd travel north to my familiar network of friends and business contacts, staying from Thursday afternoon until Sunday or Monday morning. In Bakersfield, my roommate's grueling schedule—six to seven days of 5:00 a.m. to 7:00 p.m. shifts—meant we rarely crossed paths, even when I was in town.

Bakersfield is a town dominated by two industries: agriculture and oil. It sits at the southern edge of California's Central Valley, just before the mountains that separate it from Los Angeles. The city's geography creates a peculiar prison of air: The surrounding mountains form a bowl that traps pollutants pushed south by winds from the Pacific Ocean off the Bay Area, known as the Delta Breeze. The air was so consistently thick that I lived in Bakersfield for nine months before I saw the nearby mountains— massive peaks rising three-quarters of a mile high, barely thirty miles away. I found myself retreating farther north more often, where the Delta Breeze would bring clean, fresh, cool air into the valley. The difference was stark: At night, temperatures between the two locations could vary by as much as twenty degrees.

On one of my end-of-week trips north, I got a call from my Bakersfield roommate telling me he would be leaving his job. He was heading back home to Vermont for another position. In Bakersfield, I was adrift—unfamiliar with the neighborhoods and knowing *no one* except a couple of farmers and my now-departing roommate. I had never had to find an apartment in my life, let alone figure out how to afford one on my own. While wrestling with these concerns, he dropped his bombshell: "I'm leaving Sunday. Your stuff needs to be out by Monday." I would have liked some time to figure it out and strategize, but so much for that.

So what did I do? I put it off; I sealed off having to think or deal with it for the weekend. On Monday, I left my friend's house and drove the three hours back to Bakersfield with fear, anguish, and despair. Where would I go? Could I find a place to live? Could I afford it? Could I get an apartment and move in that day?

Driving to the house, I had a short-term plan: load everything into my truck. A bed, desk, chair, set of bookshelves, entertainment center, TV, and clothes. Simple, except for the early 2000s TV, which became my nemesis. At 150 pounds, it had taken two of us to carry it in, and now I faced doing it by myself, struggling to get a grip, fearful it would drop and crash. Every attempt filled me with visions of smashed hands, crushed feet, or both. As I wrestled with this technological boulder, my frustration mounted beyond the physical and situational struggle.

I managed to get the TV into the truck without breaking it, myself, or my truck, but I was exasperated. This forced move had yanked me from my comfortable routine, a job I liked, and friends who mattered. The friends I knew and the relationships I valued were nowhere close to where I was now. The past few months of splitting my life between two regions had only deepened my isolation. Instead of putting down roots in my new community and making new relationships, I kept retreating to familiar territory, where I felt welcome and safe.

I finished packing my clothes into the cab of my truck. I climbed into the driver's seat, took a deep breath, and looked out the passenger side mirror to ensure everything in the back was secured. The pile of clothes on the front seat was so high I couldn't see out the passenger window. Thinking, *what am I going to do now?* I put my truck in drive and pulled out of the driveway, hoping for inspiration.

Bakersfield, a city of about 350,000 people in the early 2000s, had several sections of town, as most cities do. The farm where my college classmate worked, where we had lived, was south of Bakersfield, and the section of the town closest to where we lived was called the Southwest. A pretty unique name if I do say so myself! Ha!

This sector was part new homes and developments, part old homes built decades before, and had a few apartment complexes scattered throughout. The grocery store and gym I frequented were in this area, so I started driving around to find apartment complexes with vacancies. I started with the newer ones, places I thought it would be nice to live in as a young professional. The first one I saw, I drove in, thinking to myself, *This will be easy. I'll find a place, and off we go. I'll get an apartment. I need to unload all my stuff and have a place to sleep tonight.*

"Sorry, we don't have any empty units." So onto the next place I drove, a bit discouraged but not defeated.

"All we have are three-bedroom apartments." Yeah, that's too much space, and I don't know anyone who could be my roommate.

"We have a two-bedroom apartment. The deposit is $2,000, plus first and last months' rent, and the monthly rent is $1,000." Wow, I was not prepared for this, mentally or financially. Despite earning a decent salary, I hadn't budgeted or prepared to hand over nearly a month's pay in a single day. At this point, I was feeling lost. I had driven up and down the roads in the Southwest neighborhood and was striking out. I knew I wouldn't be able to keep everything in my truck for the next few days or even overnight, so I needed to figure out somewhere to put it until I could find an apartment.

As I was driving around with all my possessions in my truck, I passed Derrell's Mini Storage. Rows and rows of low-slung buildings with the traditional rolling doors for each unit. Without a plan for what to do next, I knew I had to get the stuff out of my truck. I pulled in and went to the office to see if I could get a storage unit. I had never rented, much less been in, a storage facility before. So when the clerk asked how much space I needed, I shot them a look of total loss.

"How many bedrooms of stuff do you have?" they asked.

"One," I responded, with a feeling of relief and overwhelm.

Even though it was springtime, the heat that day was relenting. Sweat poured from my head, mixing with the heavy tears leaking from my eyes as I unloaded everything but my clothes into the small garage-style unit. I was heartbroken and struggling. I was all alone. I felt like Tom Hanks's character, Chuck Noland, in the movie *Cast Away*. I was marooned on an island, struggling to survive. I was soul-searching about how to survive all alone. How do I find food, shelter, and companionship? Life was way harder in Bakersfield than it had been in Modesto. I didn't have a social network. The dairy industry was much smaller. Most of the farmers, who were much older than I, had moved to Bakersfield themselves in recent years, and, like my roommate, were working long hours day after day. And I was in no way connected to their social network. This was a reality that lasted for all eight years I lived in the area.

On Monday, I would be doing what I usually did on Mondays: driving the area, getting my bearings, stopping at farms to meet owners, and starting the process to solicit business. As a DMC, selling my consultation services was much more relationship-oriented than transactional; while there were rarely contracts, the working relationship usually lasted years. One of the toughest parts of my job was that making a "sale" often meant someone else would get fired, and while this isn't abnormal for other consultation jobs, in dairy nutrition, new business might come only every few years or even decades. My dad had a similar role to mine. One minor reason I chose not to go back to Ohio after college was that I didn't want to compete against him. I had seen him work with clients from the day he started his career until I left for California, nearly twenty years later. I knew this wasn't a career that was making sales and taking names.

What was worse about the area around Bakersfield was the number of potential clients. Even though Kern County, where Bakersfield is, had a large number of cows, there were very few farms. Only about fifty in the entire area, each averaging over three thousand cows per farm. This means if I visited five farms per day, it would only take me two weeks to see all the farms. All this to say, a day without visiting farms didn't really affect my job much!

After unloading everything, I got back into my truck and sat with the air-conditioning blowing on me full force. Now, where was I going to go? I had found a place to put my stuff, but I had nowhere to go that night. On a couple of my drives north through the heart of the city, I had seen a Hampton Inn. I didn't know much about lodging at that point, but I had stayed at Hampton Inns during college trips and one of my internships and figured it was at least a bed for the night.

I pulled up to the hotel, found a parking spot, and walked inside to see if I could get a room. The attendant asked a pretty standard question: "How many nights will you be staying?"

"Um, uh, uh, three nights," I forced out. I had no idea, and figured, *Let's start there.*

Belongings stored. A bed for a few nights was secured. Um, what should I do for dinner?

After showering and changing, I got back in my truck and set out to find dinner. This was before smartphones and AI; there was no easy way to search for everything, so I just had to wander and find a restaurant. I pulled out of the hotel and turned left onto California Avenue. I had no idea where I was going or what I would find. It was for sure an adventure, but most definitely not one I was prepared for.

I drove past building after building until I found a cluster of restaurants. Finally, I saw a sign I recognized: Outback Steakhouse. I parked and walked into the restaurant. I took a seat at the bar and ordered a beer, party of one. I sat on the stool trying to hold it all together. This was the moment I felt the most alone. No one to joke or chat with, no one to interact with—just me, a beer, and whatever game was on the television.

"Is anyone joining you?" asked the bartender.

"Nope, just me."

"Just drinking or eating?" he followed up.

"Yeah, I'm getting dinner. Can I get a menu, please?"

I had been alone in restaurants, bars, and other places before, but this was different. I was truly alone. I was in California, thousands of miles away from anyone and anything I knew, and homeless.

Alone by Design

A major contributor to homelessness is a lack of, or a breakdown in, relationships. Across cultures and communities, without connection, we're vulnerable.[5] Like a drug addict, a criminal, or someone suffering from mental illness, my walls kept me from building relationships that could have supported me, and they left me all alone. Sure, I had relationships in other places, but that didn't change the reality in Bakersfield. I'd had opportunities and chose not to develop relationships. I was being transactional rather than connecting with others.

At the bar, I slowly ate my steak, trying to take my time. I had nowhere to go and no one to go there with. Eventually, I paid my bill and got up to leave, when I saw a couple that I recognized. They were around my age or slightly older, and I had seen them several times at the gym. Definitely not enough to be friends, or even know their names. There was a moment of relief in seeing familiar faces, which was quickly replaced by the desire to cover up all the emotions of need and vulnerability.

They saw and recognized me too. We exchanged hellos and small talk, but my mind was spinning, thinking about all the judgments they must have of me. *Who goes out to dinner all alone? What kind of loser is this guy? Weird.*

My fears and insecurities about what people thought made me burn with self-consciousness. I was alone, and they knew it. I left, not even trying to make conversation, feeling a spiral of rejection, unworthiness, failure, loneliness, overwhelm, and fatigue.

I was at a low, and in that moment, something hardened inside me—every defensive wall I possessed rose at once, sealing me away from the world.

A few days later, I found an apartment not far from the restaurant where I had eaten dinner that first night. Besides the walls of my insecurity that would protect me, I now had an actual building to offer some solace.

The walls of our insecurity create a barrier to our ability to connect with others. Ultimately, this creates the feeling of being alone on an island.

Looking back, I had countless opportunities to create and build relationships and connections in Bakersfield before moving out. Despite the constraints of my industry, a few owners and dairy operators in the area were close enough to my age, and potential friendships had been within my reach. But my insecurity created walls to connecting with them, manifesting in destructive patterns: overcompensating with *intensity* as I tried to prove myself; choosing *inactivity* by avoiding return visits to dairies; displaying *insensitivity* by making a sale all about me instead of building a relationship; and ultimately choosing *isolation* by leaving town.

My fears and insecurity caused these behaviors, which were rooted in a deep sense of worthlessness, and poisoned nearly every relationship and potential connection. Interactions became fully transactional, and I learned that the walls we construct limit others' ability to connect with us. They create a barrier between the truly authentic and vulnerable self and the outside world. The feelings of overwhelm, fatigue, failure, and emotional and physical loneliness are just the results of a lack of connection.

Take, for example, that night at the Outback Steakhouse. The couple I recognized from the gym, Jacob and Tracie, would later become friends. They even tried to help me buy my first house a few years later. I could have easily opened up and shared that I was in between places and asked if they knew the area and could provide suggestions or help me in some way. Knowing them now, I think they would absolutely have helped. Even sharing that my roommate, the only other person I knew in town, had left, might have earned an invitation to hang out.

But I didn't. My fears and insecurities got the best of me, so I put my head down and pushed. I'd find ways to isolate myself, leaving town to see the friends I already had, wasting time on projects to avoid rejection, and keeping to myself, entirely insensitive to anyone else who looked like they were alone.

Those walls don't only affect others; they block authentic vulnerability and genuine connection, fueling worst-case scenarios in our minds and forcing us into self-preservation.

I now know that if I had opened up, told Jacob and Tracie I was new in town and needed help, they would not have thought less of me. They would have seen me. If I had been willing to own how I was showing up—walls six feet thick and ten feet high, strong enough to protect against the worst of natural disasters—I wouldn't have been so cold, distant, and closed off.

My walls had made me all alone on an island—one of my own creation.

4 WALLS OF INSECURITIES' IMPACT ON YOU

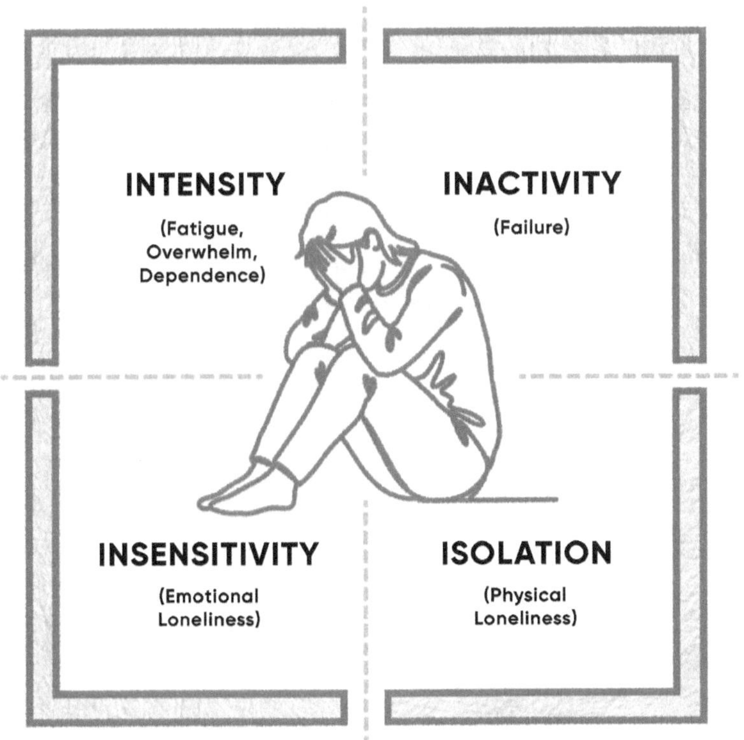

Exercise

Reflect on your Insecurity Impact Assessment results. Using those answers, note how your wall affects you.

How does *intensity* make you feel overwhelmed, dependent, or fatigued?

How does *inactivity* make you feel like a failure?

How does *insensitivity* contribute to emotional loneliness?

How does *isolation* make you feel absolutely alone?

The goal of this chapter was to expose how these walls wear us down and cut us off—how quickly they turn real connection into surface-level transactions and quiet distance. If we want to move forward, we have to stop assuming how we think we show up and start owning how others actually experience us. In chapter 4, we'll begin adding windows to those walls—because clarity changes perspective, and perspective changes the choices we make when it matters most.

PART 2

OWN HOW YOU SHOW UP TO OTHERS

PUTTING WINDOWS IN YOUR HOUSE

Taking a look in the mirror is an idiom as old as time. Or, at least as old as mirrors, which date to approximately eight thousand years ago in Anatolia. So, a long time.

Mirrors predate windows; glass windows, that is, were first rudimentarily used in the first century. With that context, it's no surprise that humans favor the mirror over the window; we have been looking at ourselves far longer than we've been peering out.

I was first introduced to the rearview-versus-windshield concept during my years as a dairy nutritionist.

Accounting, by nature, records and benchmarks costs already incurred (the rearview mirror). In contrast, forecasting projects future expenses and revenues (like a windshield).

Simply put, the mirror shows where you've been; the windshield shows where you're going. Try driving the freeway using only mirrors, and you'll create chaos for yourself and everyone around you.

The idea of mirrors and windows in leadership teaching is not new. In the classic *Good to Great*, Jim Collins references this phenomenon.

> Level 5 leaders look out the window to apportion credit to factors outside of themselves when things go well (and if they cannot find a specific person or event to give credit to, they credit good luck). At the same time, they look in the mirror to apportion responsibility, never blaming bad luck when things go poorly.
>
> The comparison leaders did just the opposite. They'd look out the window for something or someone outside themselves to blame for poor results, but would preen in front of the mirror and credit themselves when things went well. Strangely, the window and the mirror do not reflect objective reality. Everyone outside the window points inside, directly at the Level 5 leaders, saying, "He was the key; without his guidance and leadership, we would not have become a great company." And the Level 5 leader points right back out the window and says, "Look at all the great people and good fortune that made this possible: I'm a lucky guy." They're both right, of course. But Level 5s would never admit that fact.[6]

I would be remiss to discount Collins's assessment; instead, I want to add a perspective.

Collins's framing is useful; here's the extension: The mirror and the window aren't just attribution devices (blame versus credit, luck versus skill), they are development tools. The mirror reveals intention; the window reveals impact. Level 5 leaders close that gap on purpose by seeking outside perspectives and adjusting their behavior, not just apportioning credit.

Exercise: See What Others See

To make the window-and-mirror idea concrete, try this quick exercise. Imagine you have a phone with a camera nearby. Grab your phone and open up the camera application. Point the front-facing camera and screen toward you. Now make sure that your face is showing on the screen. You'll most likely look at that face and think, *I know that person. I saw that face in the bathroom mirror this morning.* You're scanning the image, recognizing the factors that make you who you are. There's a little scar, or a wrinkle, and a blemish, ah, that pimple, would it heal up already? You quickly see and acknowledge everything you're used to. Maybe you're even like my daughter and my wife, who check their makeup with this process, or my sons, who do this to check their hair. Oh, to have hair! I can say I've never used this exercise to see how shiny my head is. Now . . . take a picture. Once the camera has captured the image, open it. For my iPhone, it's in the lower-left corner.

Brace yourself! Your mind has some version of these words going through your head: *Goodness gracious, is that how I show up? My face looks distorted, my ears are misshapen, my jaw is out of line. I think something is wrong.*

> WE ONLY SEE OUR INTENTIONS THROUGH THE MIRROR, NOT THE ACTIONS OTHERS SEE THROUGH THE WINDOW.

Hate to break it to you. That is the person everyone (i.e., anyone except you) sees. The only person who saw the image you were so comfortable with was you. Everyone else sees this picture.

I first recognized this phenomenon years ago, while hosting a daily live Facebook production called Coffee Chat. This segment was a quick three-to-five-minute spot where I would share a Thought of the Day and engage with viewers. The Thought of the Day could be something like "Leadership Is a Challenge," "How to Overcome Fears," or "Less Is More." In the video, I shared the thought, and I would explain the lesson I learned or what led to that thought that day. They are archived on my YouTube channel, under the "Thought of the Day" playlist. One day, my friend Trina shared this message:

> Good morning 😊
>
> I was watching your Coffee Chat 😇 I enjoy them! If I may make one observation . . . when you record, the objects in the background are in reverse . . . if you reversed them, specifically the "love" and "faith" on the shelves, we would be able to read them straight on . . . just a small thought . . . those are powerful words that may make a difference in someone's day as they watch your chat. 😇 Have a great day!

Before Trina's note, I had no idea what the camera's mirror effect was doing. As soon as I read it, I figured out how to change the settings and unmirror the videos. What I saw rattled me at first, like the "real photo" exercise earlier. I didn't want to know the person I saw. It was uncomfortable and unnerving; the mirrored view let me hide in my intentions. Unmirroring forced me to see the version others saw, one I wasn't comfortable with. To get *Love* and *Faith* to read correctly in the background, I had to accept the misshapen, awkward image of myself. Even now, when I see the real image, I catch myself tilting my head or squaring my jaw, trying to make it look like the me I'm used to. But it never holds because that's not who I am. It's just a momentary pose.

All the efforts aside, I did grasp the bigger picture of Trina's message: The sooner I saw how I was expressing "Love" and "Faith" to others, the sooner I realized that others weren't seeing them. While I saw LOVE and FAITH, everyone else saw EVOL and HTIAF. In my heart, I wanted others to understand me.

What started as a simple private message has turned into a life lesson I return to often. I wanted those words to be readable, so whenever I'm hosting a Zoom meeting or recording a video or podcast, I make sure to unmirror my camera to see what others see. I've grown more comfortable with that view of myself than the one in the mirror. It's a simple, conscious practice to remember how people experience me. Our intentions live in the mirror; the window shows our actions. That distinction has been life-changing, and it's the core of this chapter: We only see our intentions through the mirror; others see our impact.

Window-and-Mirror T-Chart

The table below is an example of how the image we see in the mirror can differ from what others "see" or experience. It is not an exhaustive list. The mirror is our intentions. The window is what others see, their perceptions of our actions. The bridge is a way to clean our window, so we can see what they see.

Mirror (Intention)	Window (Perception)	Bridge (Alignment Shift)
Assertive	Commanding/ Unapproachable	Pair confidence with curiosity: ask questions, invite input, and use open body language.
Critical Thinking	Judgmental/ Critical of people	Separate the idea from the person: Frame critiques as "What if we tried . . . ?" instead of "That won't work."
Delegating	Abdicating/ Checked out	Clarify expectations, provide resources, and check in without micromanaging.
Transparency	Oversharing/ Creating confusion	Share what's *useful* and actionable, not everything on your mind. Anchor openness in purpose.
Motivating	Pressuring/ Micromanaging	Inspire by highlighting vision and progress, then trust people with autonomy to execute.

Assertive

Assertiveness is being direct, driven, and efficient. Recently, after speaking at a Global Leadership Conference, an audience member shared how his superior's assertive style came across as commanding, aloof, and unapproachable. The assertiveness created division rather than connection. Clarity is essential for leaders, but so is connection. A cold, insensitive approach doesn't allow for dialogue, clarification, and the feeling that *we're in this together*. Assertiveness, coupled with curiosity, can convey urgency while allowing input, collaboration, and connection.

Critical Thinking

I loved catching fireflies when I was a kid. I would pull them apart and try to understand why they glowed—curiosity that, unfortunately, ended the experiment. I'm the same with ideas: I want to collect and refine them in real time. I am a very strategic person by nature, which often leads to critical "realistic" thinking. By nature, I'm strategic, which can tip into critical, hyper-realistic thinking. For those who love to toss around ideas like fireflies on a Midwestern summer night, I can feel like the bug zapper, snuffing out anything that gets too close. My penchant for progress can come across as judgmental and critical of those with different ideas. The practice of *yes, and* is catching the firefly and letting it live—so the idea survives and sparks new ones.

Delegating

When I was sixteen, I worked for a farmer who had a health challenge. He was incapacitated for months, so I took on key responsibilities for the dairy farm. After several months of recovery, the farmer began taking back more of his responsibilities, and my tasks shifted from being key to doing busywork, such as using a power washer to clean equipment day after day. I went from feeling tremendously valued to feeling like I was wasting my time. Part of the challenge is that the key tasks were duties I had previously performed regularly at my family's dairy farm. After the third or fourth day of slipping down the totem pole, I approached the owner, frustrated, and shared, "I'm not here to do busywork; I have that to do at my own farm. Call me back when you have more valuable tasks for me."

Assigning someone a task without clear direction or expectations can seem more like a prison sentence than a growth opportunity. The people who seem not to care, then care too much, stifle creativity or intuition. While the mirror suggests empowerment, the window can display a much different picture—carelessness or abdication; giving someone busywork to appease or occupy, but nothing with meaningful value. I never got a call back! In hindsight, had the farm owner provided me with more context and made me feel genuinely valued, I probably would have worked there for years, even at sixteen.

Transparent

Enough! Yep, I'm guilty. I get on a roll and keep talking. With more information, you can make a better decision or be empowered for future decisions, right? Too often, I would share so much that I lost people long before I reached the point.

My friend Katie Quesada, a storytelling coach, says every story needs three components: context, conflict, and conclusion. Most of us overplay one and underplay another—too much context, skipped or endless conflict, or no conclusion. A proper story has the right blend of each. Learning to share appropriately helps people connect and relate more, and keeps them with you.

Craig Groeschel, in his leadership podcast, draws a helpful distinction: Leaders are obligated to tell the truth, but that doesn't mean they're obligated to tell all of it.[7] Authentic vulnerability shares what's useful and purposeful—not everything. Transparency is just enough without being too much: words chosen with purpose to build connection, not to convince or fill space. Think of it like salt; enough for flavor, not so much that it overwhelms the dish.

Motivating

Henry was one of those kids who made soccer look effortless. He was, in so many ways, a joy to coach. He had a smooth touch and always made the right pass at the right pace. He was respectful, and his teammates enjoyed being around him. He played aggressively and worked hard. The kind of player you loved to be able to use as an example of giving it everything you've got.

But he could be electrifying or absent. At first, I thought it was because he was new to our team. He had a tremendously coachable spirit, always taking a moment or two after practice to ask another coach for feedback or direction.

But then I started to put things together. At every practice or game, off in the distance, a man watched everything. He wasn't mingling with the other parents who were socializing. He was alone, with a highly intuitive, discerning look. During drills, I would see Henry glance his way, as if he were seeking validation or correction. Up to this point, the opportunity hadn't presented itself for me to speak with his dad, but I could tell he was trying to pull the strings, *willing* Henry to perform, and every look was a sign of pressure.

His dad was pressuring him and breaking him down so much to push him to be better. But it made him afraid. He was tentative. He was playing tight, thinking about every move, pass, or shot, and how his dad would respond. Not how he could help himself or his teammates win the match. By mid-season, the effect was noticeable. Henry wasn't playing to support his team and utilize his gifts; he was playing to appease his dad, even at his own detriment.

He'd hesitate on open shots or sail the shot ten feet over the goal, trying to emphatically score. He would freeze when a defender closed in, looking at the sidelines to see if his dad approved before he made a move with the ball.

His talent didn't disappear. It tightened. He had handcuffs on to keep him out of jail before he ever committed a crime.

One evening after practice, I pulled Henry aside—not as a coach correcting a player but as someone trying to understand the story beneath the behavior.

"Henry, what's going on?"

He stared at the ground, with his feet dancing back and forth.

He was lost. Partly by my question, but more so on how to answer. I shared with him that I could tell something was off, and I wanted to help him. Finally, he opened up to me. He was hesitant, and I could already put the pieces together. Then he said something a kid shouldn't have to process: "I'm not playing soccer anymore. I'm trying not to disappoint my dad."

He explained that on every car ride home, he was grilled, and every moment of the training session or match was analyzed. Every mistake was replayed. Every performance was compared.

Manufacturing pressure never leads to maximized performance; it leads to distrust and animosity. It leads to fear and paralysis. Many managers and sports coaches believe that the best way to motivate people is to ramp up the "competition," often pitting teammates and friends against each other. Competition should be internal, not external. Be better than you were yesterday. Motivation without a link to vision, personal or corporate, seems fulfilling only to the motivator. It can appear like micromanagement and force rather than inspiration and belief—encourage rather than challenge. Call people to achieve a vision rather than demanding they perform to impress.

Intention Versus Impact: How Others Experience You

Through Maxwell Leadership's Executive Circle, my coach, Rick VanDermyden, guided me through a 360-degree review that changed how I saw myself.

Though I knew what 360-degree reviews were, I'd never done one, and it proved to be the truest mirror. If you've done a 360-degree review, you understand the process. If not, here's the short version: You answer fifty to sixty questions about your leadership, work style, and relationships. First, you rate yourself, then peers, supervisors, and direct reports answer the same questions about you. The results are compiled and compared, revealing where your self-view aligns with, or diverges from, how others experience you.

I had a similar experience to what I shared with you when I took a picture of myself with my phone. "That's not me. That's not what I look like. Those are not my intentions." It was humbling. The clearest theme from the assessment was blunt: *I was out for myself. It was about my accolades. My goals. Me, me, me.* As I read it, my heart dropped. That wasn't how I saw myself. I didn't have some grand self-serving agenda. I wasn't looking for the next thing to accomplish or possession to attain and boast about. I was head down doing work; you know, the intensity thing we talked about earlier.

I had a lot of rectifying to do.

Tasha Eurich, in her book *Insight*, shares the Prism Effect, which describes self-awareness as a combination of personal mirrors and the windows of perspective from others. As she describes it, self-awareness is not a single truth; it's a complex interweaving of our own views and others' opinions of us.

This is so much more of the overall picture than the simplicity Jim Collins shared in the book *Good to Great*. "Owning How You Show Up to Others" means accepting that your mirror is not their window. Over time, when we don't ask others what they see, our view gets cloudy or obstructed.

When the Windshield Gets Dirty

Imagine a summer day: You're driving down the road in the Midwest, bugs thick in the air, and every few seconds—splat— another hits the glass. Where I live in the Pacific Northwest, farms and fields make bug season just as real. It's pretty standard for windshields to collect the same steady splats. On long trips, the windshield, which shows you where you are going, can get so covered that it's nearly impossible to see. It is starting to fail. Eventually, you have to do two things: a quick pass of the windshield with your wipers, which can work as a short-term fix when buildup is light, or a deeper clean—a squeegee at the gas station or a full car wash—to restore a clear view.

Keep in mind that the view in the mirrors rarely changes. Bugs don't hit the rearview mirror, which is inside your vehicle, and the side mirrors point backward. Still, I've seen windshields so covered in bug guts that people seem to drive by mirrors alone, oblivious to the mess right in front of them.

In this metaphor, our relationship experiences with others are the bugs. Sometimes, no bugs are flying around—the windshield is clear, everything's good, and everyone's happy with how you're interacting with them. Other times—summer where I live, or spring—there are a lot of bugs, and it's "splat, splat, splat."

Those bugs are telling us something; they wouldn't bother us if they weren't obstructing our view. If we just get used to it, we crane our necks and look side to side and up and down, without accounting for the splats. They receive feedback, as I did with the 360-degree assessment, and simply discount it. Checking their mirrors, they think everything is fine. They might even shift around in the driver's seat, avoiding the obstruction right in front of their eyes. At worst, they stop looking out the windshield. They ignore feedback from others. They isolate themselves or create situations in which people are reluctant to alert them, while they remain oblivious. These people often think, *I'm just going to look in the mirror. I like what I see in the mirror. My intentions are good; I'm a good person—and I look good too!*

The next thing they know, they hit a wall, and their world comes crashing down. The windshield is shattered. The protected mirrors are cracked, and the view they see now is wildly distorted. And there might be some massive collateral damage.

Exercise: 360-Degree View

Do a 360-degree review—evaluate how you show up to different people at different times.

Here is a simple way to conduct a light 360 if you're not doing a full assessment.

Ask two to three people with whom you work or regularly interact.

1. How do you see me through our relationship "window"?
2. How does that make you feel?
3. How can I act differently to improve your experience of me?

What patterns do you notice? Are people willing to answer the questions, or are they hesitant? Are the answers specific or vague?

If people are engaging and sharing some hard truths, your "windshield" is most likely pretty clean. Nice work. If not, then get to a "car wash" ASAP! This is your sign to get a more in-depth assessment before the mirror shatters.

When the window is clean, the real work begins: noticing how we show up in different rooms with different people. In chapter 5, we'll move from seeing clearly to acting differently, mapping where our insecurities cloud the view and where they lift, so we can build consistency without losing authenticity.

SHOWING UP DIFFERENTLY IN DIFFERENT SITUATIONS

During my sophomore year at Cornell, I jumped at the chance to study abroad at Lincoln University in New Zealand, a partner school offering semester-long exchanges. I'd learned about the program as a freshman and set my sights on the following spring.

In total, seven students joined the study abroad program, all connected to the dairy science program, despite very different majors. Two of my fraternity brothers joined the trip. The familiarity and comfort helped, but the distance from home stripped away my routines and forced me to face some of the personality challenges that had been straining my relationships.

I've learned since then that the class selections in study abroad programs vary tremendously. In some cases, there is a very rigid structure that helps students acclimate to a new culture or language; in others, it is up to you to make the most of your experience. I was afforded a bit of both. Class selection was wide open: an animal production course with a midsemester trip to North Island to dairy and sheep farms, a sports tourism class—whew, I had no idea what I signed up for—and a business course—each showing me systems far different from those I was used to in the United States.

In sports tourism, I met several other US students, many from Colorado State University, another Lincoln partner. A few of us planned a hiking trip to Arthur's Pass in the Southern Alps, the route linking the South Island's east and west coasts.

Five of us were committed—two from Colorado State, one from Purdue, and one from Germany. Several were experienced mountaineers and outdoor enthusiasts; this was my first trip ever! This Midwestern Ohio kid had never walked a trail carrying a backpack full of gear, much less climbed to a peak jutting out of the earth more than six thousand feet high. For reference, Ohio's highest point is Campbell Hill; yes, a hill, a whopping 1,549 feet (472 meters).

When my feet hit the train station platform at Arthur's Pass Railway Station before we started our climb, I was already at nearly twice Ohio's high point—about 737 meters—still more than a thousand meters below our ultimate destination, Avalanche Peak.

I'd chosen to study abroad for moments like this—living and learning on the other side of the world was exhilarating and adventurous. I didn't know yet which lessons would stick, which I'd resist, and which perspectives I would only recognize later.

Most international students arrived solo; I arrived with a Cornell cohort. I hadn't spent much time with them in my previous three college semesters. We were friendly, but not really close, and I often felt like an outsider inside the group. I even clashed with a couple of people when I couldn't keep my intensity in check.

This hiking trip promised challenge and novelty. One of the more experienced members of the group mapped out and assembled our weekend itinerary. We would take the bus from campus to Christchurch and board the TranzAlpine train to Arthur's Pass. After arriving and refueling, we would begin our ascent with the intention of summiting in the afternoon. We would then descend the other side of the peak and spend the night in one of the huts located along several of the trails in the Arthur's Pass National Park.

Having never been on a trip like this, the week before I set out for Christchurch, I found a sporting goods store where I could get the essentials: a backpack, a sleeping bag, and a headlamp. A couple of other guys were well outfitted with the other items we might need.

As we left town, our spirits were high. The weather for late March in the New Zealand Alps was pleasant and fall-like. Highs in the mid-sixties Fahrenheit and lows in the lower forties. Not so hot as to be bothersome, and not so cold as to endure freezing temperatures. A light mist was falling, but the reports were that this system would pass shortly before we were to summit. We should have great hiking weather and be able to see the peak and the surrounding terrain well.

The trail we were taking, Scotts Track, is just over two miles with about 3,400 feet of elevation gain—solidly "hard," even for experienced climbers. The website Alltrails.com describes it this way:

> This is a very steep and challenging climb to the Avalanche Peak summit (1883) in Arthur's Pass, suitable for well-equipped people with previous back-country tramping experience. It starts with a beautiful but strenuous walk through the woods, finishing with climbing on and over rocks, and provides spectacular views on the way up and down. Expect

steep and rugged terrain. Even if you don't make it to the summit, you can still see the beautiful panorama and glacier. This route can also be made into a loop by returning on the more southern Avalanche Peak trail. Please note that this is a dangerous area with avalanche potential, steep drop-offs, and uncertain weather.

My nineteen-year-old self never read that description, but even if I had, I don't think it would have changed my mind.

True to the description, the trail was steep and wet, slowing progress, but our timing was not affected. We had plenty of time to reach the summit, then descend to the Crow River Valley and Crow Hut before dark.

As we progressed toward the peak, our spirits rose in anticipation of the views ahead once we cleared the dense, tree-engulfed trail. Once we reached the tree line—the elevation at which trees don't grow and the landscape is all rock—we would be able to see the surrounding valleys.

Above the tree line, we found only heavy clouds and fog. We were disappointed, but committed. We had climbed for just under two hours, and we kept going. There was so much more to the hike. There was never a thought of turning back; we had come this far, and our route home lay over the peak.

We proceeded, transitioning from the wet, vegetation-lined trail crisscrossed with roots, over and under the broken trail from years of travelers, to pure rock. This made the walking easy, but we were completely exposed to the wind. We had completed roughly half of our hike to the peak when we transitioned to the next terrain.

Every once in a while, as we made the final approaches, we thought the clouds might clear. The rain had subsided, but the cloud cover and fog remained. We thought the clouds would clear because every few minutes, the sun would peek through and beam down bright, warming rays.

Finally reaching the peak, we set our packs aside and gathered for a group picture. We were sweaty and wet but felt accomplished and glad to reach the milestone. Then, just over my left shoulder, I could feel the warmth of the sun on the side of my face and warming me through my rain jacket. I turned, and the clouds had cleared. I could see down the valley where the Crow Hut was and where we were going. Just as I was taking it all in, another guy called out to the group as the clouds had cleared in another direction. Just as the view disappeared at another angle, you could see an entirely different perspective.

We stood there for fifteen or twenty minutes, taking it all in, looking and adjusting. What had been completely hidden just an hour before was now visible in incremental portions. We never experienced a full panoramic view, but we saw everything in snippets, shifting partial clarity. If the cloud cover and overcast skies had stayed, our view would have been entirely different. Yet they opened and revealed the beauty of the terrain below and beyond.

Our lives mirror the clouds that day. We show up differently in the relationship where our insecurity is most triggered. Our actions and responses—the walls we put up and stand behind— hide the beauty within us. All the sights on the other side of the clouds were there the entire time, but the dense mist kept them hidden. The overcast skies kept the sun from providing warmth and comfort. Our walls keep us from being seen and from seeing others.

In contrast, there are days with clear blue skies when we can see everything. When our insecurity isn't triggered, our demeanor and actions align. The walls of our insecurities have windows;

people can see our inner selves, and we let our inner selves be seen too.

In cloudy moments, we're tempted to stop at the tree line, but the horizon only appears if we keep climbing.

No doubt, if I compared my experience with others who have summited Avalanche Peak, our experiences would be vastly different. It could have been clear and sunny for their summit, snowy and blowing, or rainy and cloudy. Yet the mountains and underlying geographical formations have been the same since I set foot on the peak over twenty-five years ago. Sure, surfaces shift—trees have grown, died, or changed, avalanches and fire have hit some areas—but the underlying structure remains the same.

People are the same. In some relationships, with those who value us, where we feel comfortable, appreciated, and secure, we show up one way. In others, when we feel triggered, under-valued, provoked, criticized, afraid, doubting, vulnerable, or nervous, we show up in entirely different ways. At times, we see and understand the difference and reasoning; at others, we are entirely unaware. And rather than confront that gap, some people construct a protective alter ego, a version of themselves designed to avoid the discomfort of the dichotomy altogether. When that happens, the true self never shows up.

Just as the clouds move to reveal beautiful views, recognizing our walls—how they block us from connecting with others—and choosing to accept them reveals our true selves.

Circle of Ownership

Let me introduce a concept: the Circle of Ownership. It represents the movement from fragmented relationships—where insecurity shapes how we show up—to wholeness, where we own how others experience us and integrate their perspectives. Integration doesn't erase our core identity. A desk made of wood is still essentially the same as the tree from which it was made. Yet the wood has transformed into a fine, purposeful piece of furniture.

THE CIRCLE OF OWNERSHIP

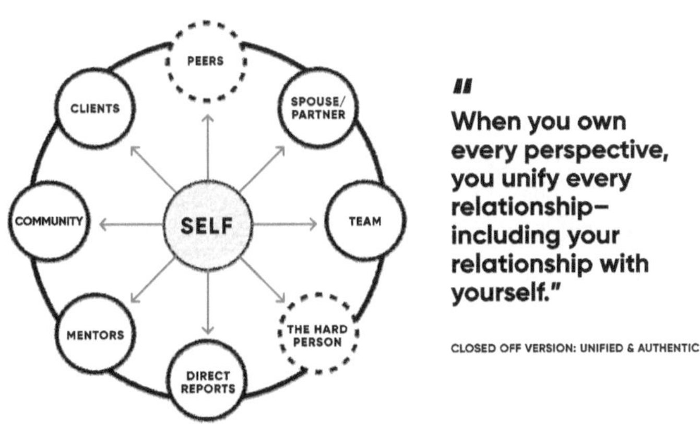

Evaluating our Circle of Ownership, we can exist in two ways: closed or open. When we are closed (represented by the dashed perimeter), we reject others' vantage points, viewpoints, or perspectives. When open, we accept how others experience us and show up as our authentic selves. Quick reminder from the last chapter: By "authentic," I mean the real you, not the walled ego, and "authentic vulnerability" is sharing in ways that deepen connection.

As with the window-and-mirror exercise, reality isn't what you see in the mirror—it's what others see through the window. The goal is to move from a fragmented "alter ego" to a unified self by taking ownership of how people actually experience you. This happens when we invite, accept, and *work with* others' perspectives (not just pretend to accept them). That ownership closes the gap between intention and impact.

Here is how it can play out:

- **Admit you're wrong.** Clarity beats defensiveness. Being wrong isn't weakness or defeat; it means someone's experience didn't match your intent, and you're willing to accept their vantage point. If I had stood at the top of Avalanche Peak and been indignant that the cloudy view was the only view, I would have missed the beauty in other directions.
- **Discover why others perceive you that way.** Don't stop at acceptance—*mine for the truth*. Seeking truth is not feel-good fluff; it's rigorous, evidence-based work. The truth—wow, it's crazy even to document this—does not necessarily conform to your beliefs. The truth is what holds *regardless of beliefs*. It's born in facts and recorded accounts from multiple sources and perspectives. As you seek others' perceptions, you start to piece together a fuller panorama, just as I did that day atop Avalanche Peak.
- **Analyze where insecurity changes your behavior.** Are you open or closed? If you're open, there are windows in your walls of insecurity. If you are closed, the walls are rigid, and you are in complete protection mode, like boarded-up windows preparing for a hurricane. Notice when you switch: One day, there are beautiful homes with light shining in; the next day, everything is closed off, fearful of the potential damage from high winds, sideways rain, and a rising tide.

If insecurities drive your presence, authenticity can't. When you own the full circle—intentions, actions, and others' experience of you—you live and lead as your authentic self.

The Rest of the Story

(An Homage to Paul Harvey)[8]

After summiting the peak, taking in all the sights and getting a roll's worth of pictures, we found the west-side trail to descend the peak to Crow Hut, where we would lodge for the night. The ascent trail was well marked and worn; by contrast, the trail down the ridge was not! It was guess and hope for the best. Jeremy, our lead guide, used a map and a compass to guide us along the most logical route down a ridge: west. This made it easy to decide which direction to go. However, it surely did not give us the "best, most logical path." Simple in theory, not in practice.

As we were trying to get on the trail along the ridge, we got to the point where we knew we had to head toward the bottom of the valley. We needed a switchback trail that would weave us down the slope to the hut some three thousand feet below. It just didn't exist. The shortest distance between the two points was straight down a hill of rock. Not solid granite, like you might have seen at Yosemite National Park in California. More a jumble of loose rocks—softball to soccer-ball size—that roll under your feet. The backside of Avalanche Peak lived up to its name.

When there was no better option, we committed. One by one, we stepped off the ridge and started down the slope. To give context, the slope dropped roughly a thousand feet at a pitch steeper than a double black diamond. Insane! But we weren't skiing down this slope; we were attempting to walk. In reality, we sat down shortly after leaving the ridge and slid the entire way down on our backpacks. Highly efficient, but because of the rolling rock and the length of the slope, if we had lost control, there would be no stopping.

Luckily, we all made it down, and once we composed ourselves, we stared back up the slope, now swallowed by clouds. This "shortcut" left us with just under a mile to the hut. We had planned to split up—some in the hut, some in tents, since five in the hut would be a little cramped. But that isn't what happened. The hut was already occupied! Another group with the same idea had already "reserved" the hut for the night. A couple of us could squeeze in; the rest braved it and slept under the stars or in tents.

It didn't rain overnight, and no one got wet. The next day, the weather was seasonably warm, perfect for the river hike to the highway that traverses the island and leads back to Christchurch—and our final challenge: getting back to campus.

Hitchhiking in New Zealand is neither illegal nor uncommon, unlike in the United States. And that was our plan for the two-hour return. When I was all in on this part of the excursion, I assumed that two or three of us would ride together. Safety in numbers. Well, it started that way. The first two guys, Jeff and Dat, caught a ride within a few minutes, leaving three of us. We figured that as quickly as they had gotten a ride, the rest of us would too.

Nope.

We waited. And waited.

This was 1999. None of us had a cell phone.

After an hour, we knew we would have to get creative. Numerous cars had passed. Maybe they didn't have room for all of us. We decided that two would hide while one flagged rides.

Sure enough, not five minutes later, a truck stopped. Surprisingly, this gentleman noticed all three of us, but he could

only take one. I went alone. Obviously, I made it back. Not
without a bit of surprise, when about ten minutes into the drive,
the driver reached into the glove compartment and offered me
some weed. I kindly passed on the offer. First and last hitchhike.

Exercise: "The Open Versus Closed Reflection"

Prompt Questions for Personal or Group Use

1. When do I feel most at ease, open, and connected to
    others? Who am I with?
2. When do I feel guarded, defensive, or performative?
    Who am I with?
3. What insecurity might be influencing those shifts?
4. How could I take ownership—listening to how others
    perceive me—so I can close the gap between those two
    versions of myself?

••◆••

In this chapter, you saw how context changes how you show
up—clear skies versus clouds, open versus closed—and why
inviting other perspectives into your Circle of Ownership matters.
Awareness is the starting point, not the finish line. In chapter
6, we move from awareness to ownership: letting light through
your window, leading with authentic vulnerability, and owning
the impact you have on others.

OWN WHAT OTHERS SEE THROUGH THE WINDOW

A couple of years ago, at a Christmas Eve service with my family, the ushers handed out electric candles. I understood the practical reasons—wax drips and causes havoc with carpet and other fabrics. And some insurance companies balk at the idea of open flames inside a building, especially with kids holding them—but it still hit me with disdain.

The electric candles they passed out looked like the typical item you'd see—a wax candle about six inches long. Instead of a wick, there was a lightbulb at the top, and a switch at the base.

This is what hurt me: From the time I was very young, every candle-lighting service handed out real candles at the door, with a circular paper disk about halfway up to keep wax from dripping onto your hand. We would hold them through the service until the lighting.

The heat from our hands would warm the wax, and if your hands were hot and sweaty enough—which was usually the case because I was inevitably wearing some kind of sweater and the fully packed room was warmer than usual—the wax would become malleable. That tactile memory felt like a small rite of passage. Seeing my sons with plastic candles, I felt a loss—until a deeper lesson emerged.

If you're unfamiliar with the tradition of a candle-lighting worship service, let me walk you through it. Usually, at the end of the service, the song "O Holy Night" is sung.

Right before the song is sung, the lights in the auditorium are dimmed. The ethereal darkness and warmth create a ceremonial, hallowed moment. At this time, with candles ready, the lighting process begins. With electric candles, everything is self-contained: Flip the switch, and the bulb lights.

> This traditional carol originated in France in 1843, when the parish priest tasked the poet Placide Cappeau with writing a poem to celebrate the renovation of the church organ for Christmas. The original composer was a friend of his, Adolphe Adam, a well-known Jewish composer of ballets and operas. Because of the author's and composer's mixed-faith traditions, many French churches banned it from services. However, due to its popularity and moving sentiments, it was still sung in homes and other gatherings. The song reached the United States in the mid-1850s and soon became a symbol of Christian faith and the abolitionist movement—a carol for faith and freedom. It became a Christmas Eve tradition when it was part of the first-ever radio broadcast in 1906.[9]

With traditional wax-and-wick candles, it is different—and relational. The process usually starts with a central candle, often from a ceremonial candle that adorns the decor. From here, light cascades from a lit candle to an unlit candle down every row. Slowly and systematically, light starts to overtake the room.

Each person along the line tilts their unlit candle to accept the flame from another lit candle. As the unlit wick dips into the fire, it ignites. One by one, a candle is lit and passes its light to another.

Within minutes, the once-dark room is illuminated by flickering light from "real" candles. Each small flame gives off light and heat, and together, they transform the room into a space navigable with light. The tiny flames give off a warming sensation that further accentuates the experience.

Once the carol is over, the candles are extinguished, and the house lights come on for the end of the event.

At less than four minutes, the ceremony is one of my favorite Christian traditions—with a lesson that lingers. When one candle lights another, it doesn't diminish or grow weaker. Together, they create a larger, brighter flame.

Just as one candle does not grow dim by lighting another, neither do we when we empower, celebrate, or mentor another person. Owning our impact doesn't diminish us; it makes us more fully human.

As a lit candle passes its flame, our actions impact and affect others. Owning that impact moves us beyond hiding or minimizing. When we recognize our influence, we start to understand our actions have consequences, good and bad.

A CANDLE DOES NOT GET WEAKER WHEN LIGHTING ANOTHER CANDLE.

Presence to Ownership

I vividly remember when this clicked for me at the Maxwell Exchange in West Palm Beach, Florida. The annual event is limited to about 120 people from diverse backgrounds, experiences, and professions, and has been hosted by John Maxwell for over twenty years. This was my second time attending, but my first time without my wife. Having attended more than five events in two years with John and his Leadership Foundation, the event felt part reunion and part new introductions.

As I entered the hotel ballroom where the day's events were held, I felt this spirit come over me: *Your energy has an impact.* I had this moment and recognized its genuine truth.

Years earlier, a peer in our network marketing organization told me that my intensity, demeanor, and presence changed a room, but I blew it off. I couldn't see it in myself or believe it until that November day in 2020.

That morning, the message was finally received. In that moment, I came to grips with the idea of ownership. I could do as I had done for years and dismiss the idea that I could affect others, or I could own it. And I chose to own it.

Owning it was the first step in understanding how the walls of insecurity show up and create barriers in my relationships with others. Conversations the day before helped me lean into my gifts to serve others. While my insecurity told me I needed to protect my soul, spirit, and purpose, my soul, spirit, and purpose spoke to me: "Serve."

As I walked to my table, I pondered how I could serve others. What was something I was gifted with, passionate about, and excited to do? It was right then and there that I conceived what I would go on to pursue for the next seven years.

I didn't have the answers yet, but I was willing to ask the questions. I was willing to try, with the intention that when my youngest son graduated from high school in just over seven years, I would be on the path to a profession that gave me life, supported my family and my greatest purpose, and gave my brother Joel's life purpose.

In part, you are reading what arose in me that morning—a desire born of the understanding that when a candle lights another, it does not grow weaker. Accepting how I show up in rooms—how I interact, encourage, and lead—extends beyond me; it is significant and impactful.

ZILJOTS: The Tetris of Authenticity

The computer game *Tetris* was developed in the early 1980s by Alexey Pajitnov, a Russian computer scientist working at the Dorodnitsyn Computing Centre of the Soviet Academy of Sciences. The game was modeled after a traditional puzzle game, pentominoes. In pentominoes, five differently shaped pieces are arranged to fit within a box. The name *Tetris* comes from the alteration Alexey made to have the pieces, tetrominoes, make shapes of four connected squares.

Each *Tetris* shape is called a *tetromino*, and each has a corresponding letter in the English alphabet: *Z, I, L, J, O, T, S*. On a computer screen or, later, Nintendo Game Boy, the shapes would descend from the top of the screen to the bottom, where they would become fixed and immovable once they hit the bottom. While descending, you can adjust the orientation of the shape to align it with other shapes to create the box structure. Once a box (a row horizontally across the screen) is made, it disappears, and the shapes start descending faster. The score is based on the number of rows completed.

The game falls apart when a piece lands in the wrong spot. A *J* is not an *L*, and an *O* is not an *I*. Placed in the wrong location, a game piece clogs the stack and disrupts the flow of the game. That pressure and uncertainty about where to send the next tetromino can cause the player to stall, speed up, overcorrect, get frustrated, or quit. Either way, the outcome is the same: The game wins.

Now imagine the same pressure to perform at school, at work, or in relationships. We respond the same way. We stall (Inactivity), move faster (Intensity), get frustrated and lash out (Insensitivity), or quit (Isolation).

Each tetromino has the same number of connected squares (four), but the arrangement and purpose of each are different. The arranger who succeeds at *Tetris* has to acknowledge, admit, and accept that each piece has different attributes and functions; yet, there is a place for all in the game.

Authentic Vulnerability

I see this dynamic in teams and organizations. The leader or coach can move, direct, or position individuals into complementary roles to achieve a desired goal. The leader is creating a box with each piece. The more effectively and efficiently they do this, the more the group can accomplish and reach its desired goal or mission.

The person who learns to know and value their specific gifts learns that they can influence others. Owning that does not take away from anyone, just as lighting one candle does not dim another's flame. In *Tetris*, the game only advances when one piece connects with and complements another.

Owning your impact does not diminish or weaken you; it makes you more fully human. As outlined in chapter 4, by *authentic vulnerability*, I mean authentically owning and vulnerably accepting yourself exactly as you are, and sharing in ways that deepen connection. When you accept your unique gifts, your puzzle piece fits in the right spot, and your light doesn't dim by sharing it. And that choice shapes how you show up.

"Showing up" is how you carry yourself—body language, tone, attitude—and it shifts depending on who we are with, the level of trust, and the circumstances. When insecurity is triggered, our walls—the armor we use to protect our fears and insecurities—change how we show up.

When we feel safe, the armor stays in its case. Learning to spot those spikes lets us choose vulnerability, and that's what enables real connection.

Accepting our fears and insecurities helps us see how they shape our actions. Guarding ourselves against harm is instinctive, but when we allow fear to lead, we keep our light hidden. For me, given my intensity, the gap between reclusive and overbearing is narrow; the middle ground is a genuine, authentic presence.

Being genuine and authentic is not the same as saying, "This is who I am—take it or leave it." That stance is pure arrogance. It's arrogant to assume others simply have to deal with us as we are. No one would walk into a home, see a beautifully finished wood floor, and call it fake because it lacks bark; we expect the planks to be milled, sanded, and finished.

EMPOWER YOURSELF BY ACCEPTING WHO YOU TRULY ARE.

When we are at ease and care for those we interact with—seeking to appreciate rather than to prove—we show up differently. We become the wax-and-wick candle that can ignite others without losing anything. Allowing the walls of our insecurities to dictate our actions is like believing that lighting someone else's candle will extinguish ours. As we've discovered, it doesn't work that way.

Feeling free to share our light helps us quickly recognize others' unique greatness and find ways to connect and engage. In *Tetris*, pieces complement each other; connection works the same way when we engage with curiosity and compassion—not to get or prove anything, but to serve and understand others.

Through these connections, the truth that everyone has value comes alive, despite the ever-present questions our insecurities raise: Am I good enough? Do I have value? Do I belong? New people enter our lives every day: How we consistently show up is the difference between rocky and fruitful relationships.

The key is to be ourselves—the self who isn't intimidated by what we aren't and isn't trying to impress others by what we think we are—choosing authentic vulnerability and lowering the walls of insecurity to connect. This is how we build meaningful relationships. We go wrong when we center ourselves instead of empathy and curiosity for others. We get it right when we seek to serve and connect because we know we have value, and we accept others' value.

Exercise: Lighting Another Candle

Owning your impact means sharing your light—it doesn't diminish you.

Purpose
Identify how you show up to others, how your unique "light" connects or disconnects, and how to own your influence through authenticity and vulnerability.

Part 1—The Candle Reflection

Recall the two candle experiences: the *electric candle*, self-contained and controlled, and the *wax-and-wick candle*, relational and interdependent.

1. Which kind of candle most reflects how you tend to show up right now?
    - Do you rely on your own internal "switch," avoiding dependence or collaboration?
    - Or do you tilt toward others—allowing your light to spread and be strengthened through connection?
2. In one sentence, describe what your "light" brings into a room. Example: "My light brings energy and optimism—but sometimes heat without warmth."
3. Think of a recent situation when you shared your light. What changed—both in you and in others?

Part 2—Own What Others See Through the Window

Your energy has an impact.

Just as I realized at the Maxwell Exchange event, my demeanor, tone, and presence created an atmosphere. I encourage you to reflect on times and situations when your presence impacted a room.

Prompt:

- How do people experience me when I enter a room?
- What emotion, pace, or posture do I carry?
- What do I want them to experience instead?

Setting	How I Show Up	Desired Impact
Family/Home		
Work/Team		
Friends/ Community		

Part 3—The *Tetris* of Authenticity (ZILJOTS)

Each tetromino has four connected squares—but each fits differently.

1. List your personal tetromino pieces:
   - **Z:** A zigzag strength—something that makes you adaptable or creative.
   - **I:** Your "straight piece"—a consistent gift or discipline.
   - **L:** A piece that sometimes feels awkward or misunderstood but serves a key role.
   - **J:** A complementary strength that balances others.
   - **O:** Your steady, grounded side.
   - **T:** A talent that connects or bridges others.
   - **S:** A piece of you that surprises people.
2. For each shape, write one word or phrase that describes how it shows up in you.
3. Circle the pieces you tend to hide or undervalue.
4. Ask: *What would happen if I accepted and used those pieces fully?*

Part 4—The Four Walls Check

We stall, speed up, lash out, or quit.

Think about how your insecurity walls appear when your pieces don't seem to fit.

Wall	How It Shows Up for Me
Intensity (pushing, forcing)	
Inactivity (stalling, freezing)	
Insensitivity (closing empathy)	
Isolation (withdrawing)	

Using the results of the Insecurity Impact Assessment and the wall you lean against most, what truth or action could lower that wall next time?

Part 5—Ask and Illuminate

When one candle lights another, the room grows brighter.

Ask three people close to you this question: "What's one thing I do that amazes or inspires you?"

Record their responses below:

Person	Their Response	What It Reveals About My Light

Look for repeated words or themes. Those are clues to your most powerful light—the one others already see through the window.

Part 6—Integrate and Act

Reflect on these questions to close:

1. What piece of your authentic self have you been hiding?
2. Where will you intentionally share your light this week?
3. Who around you needs to see your genuine warmth and not just your intensity?
4. What wall of insecurity will you lower to connect more deeply?

A CANDLE DOESN'T GET WEAKER BY LIGHTING ANOTHER.

IT SIMPLY REVEALS HOW STRONG ITS FLAME ALREADY WAS.

In this chapter, you learned to own your impact—sharing your light without dimming it, inviting perspective, and leading with authentic vulnerability. In chapter 7, we'll turn that clarity into action: finding your sweet spot, bringing out the best in others, and using the BEST framework to serve with skill and timing.

BRING OUT THE BEST IN YOURSELF AND OTHERS (SHOOT YOUR SHOT)

My family relocated to Washington from California in the summer of 2009. We had attempted to move the summer before but couldn't find a house that fit our needs. We punted, and the $8,000 gap between our offer and the seller's price turned out to be one of the greatest gifts my wife and I have ever received.

As part of the move, I kept my California nutrition consulting clients and traveled back one week per month. The other three weeks, I worked for a firm that consulted with dairy farms and feedlots across the United States, focused on commodity pricing and procurement. We helped farmers buy corn, soybean meal, and other feed ingredients and coordinated delivery to feed their animals.

I had worked with the firm for a couple of years through mutual clients, and the relationship was strong. Knowing I had to find something meaningful to fill those other three weeks of the month made the career pivot feel energizing.

The 2008 financial fallout had crushed the dairy industry, and my heart and passion were fading. I had lost business. I kept grinding, doing the same thing, hoping for different results, all while watching my confidence slide. Was I even good at my job? I needed off the hamster wheel.

I had no clue what my "best" was, much less where and how to deploy it. I was doing more and feeling less.

Best isn't a title—it's a choice you make in a moment. You bring out the best when you find your sweet spot and help others stand in theirs. This chapter is about shooting your shot: naming what you do uniquely well, accepting that it's enough, serving so others can win, and mastering timing. That's the BEST framework we'll use to turn potential into performance.

Best shows up when potential becomes performance. It's the moment you do what you uniquely do, and help others do the same.

If you've felt stuck, aware of your potential but unclear how to use it, you're not alone. I've been there, aware I had potential but unsure how to express or harness it, let alone understand how to bring it out in others. As Claude Silver, chief heart officer of VaynerX, writes in *Be Yourself at Work*, "If we can just catch a glimpse of our potential, we might never again settle for anything less."[10]

Fulfillment came when I focused on my sweet spot and helped others to step into theirs. That's where your "best" lives. Let's find it and shoot your shot.

Finding the Sweet Spot

The legendary coach John Wooden served as UCLA's basketball coach from 1948 to 1975. Many—well, at least *I*—have noted Coach Wooden as one of the greatest basketball coaches ever. In his twenty-seven years of coaching, he never had a losing season, compiling an overall record of 620 wins and 147 losses. His teams won ten NCAA men's basketball championships in a twelve-year span from 1964 to 1975. In total, he coached and developed four Naismith Memorial Basketball Hall of Fame players: Gail Goodrich, Jamaal Wilkes, Bill Walton, and Kareem Abdul-Jabbar.

Regardless of the previous year's success or the team's experience, Coach Wooden began every season with two iconic moves. First, before they ever ran a drill or started fitness conditioning, he taught every athlete, even his perennial stars, how to put on their socks. Yes, the thing most people mastered as toddlers was being reviewed to his seven-foot-tall superathletes on how to correctly put on socks to prevent blisters. Coach Wooden understood that small details, repeated faithfully, compound into excellence.

Second, he discovered where each player was their BEST and engineered the team to express its collective best; a championship recipe.

After socks, he would watch them play, studying each player, the combinations that worked, and the spots on the court where their strengths showed up.

Maybe it was the corner shot that only one player could hit with consistency. Maybe it was the rebounder who grabbed a missed shot and kicked the ball to the point guard with perfect timing and efficiency. Maybe it was the player who helped teammates find their spots so they could play their best.

Coach Wooden evaluated collectively, not just individually. One season, he even benched his most talented player, simply because the team performed better without him on the court.

He invested many hours and days into practice, watching and taking notes to understand each player's value to the team and how the group could excel as a team.

Eventually, he gathered the team, laid out his findings, and guided each player to a place on the court, their "sweet spot," while encouraging teammates to learn and chronicle where others were at their best.

Coach Wooden empowered his players with clear direction, high expectations, and a unified purpose, helping each player bring out their BEST so the team could do the same.

Unlocking potential meant placing players in their sweet spots, shooting, passing, rebounding, or contributing to the team in other ways. For some, that meant starting and filling the box score; for others, it meant a vital reserve role. Swen Nater is a prime example.

At UCLA, Swen's primary role was to develop his senior teammate, Hall of Famer Bill Walton. Bill was a three-time consensus All-American and Player of the Year for the Bruins, who averaged over twenty points per game.

Bill and Swen were arguably the best two centers in college basketball, but because they played the same position, they rarely shared the court. Swen's role was to help Bill improve at every practice, proof that a Hall of Fame career can be built as a backup when your sweet spot is developing others. Coach Wooden positioned him to bring out the BEST in Bill and the entire UCLA team.

Others recognized Swen's ability too. He was a first-round draft pick in the 1973 National Basketball Association Draft, a two-time league All-Star, and the first player to win Rookie of the Year without ever starting a collegiate game.

Wooden's championship recipe was simple: put people in their sweet spots and help them bring out the BEST in each other.

Before we get into tools, let's call out the pattern you just saw in Wooden's story: know your sweet spot, accept that it's enough, serve in a way that helps others win, and master timing. That's the BEST framework we'll use from here.

BEST Framework

BEST stands for **B**e Aware, That's **E**nough, **S**erve, and **T**iming. It's a simple way to turn potential into performance, yours and your teams.

Be Aware

At the end of the previous chapter, there was an exercise to ask three people you know, trust, and respect to share with you what you are great at when you're in your "sweet spot."

Being aware is knowing your unique gift and naming it. Everyone has a way to offer value to their team—the people around them. If you're a basketball player, it might be shooting baskets, dribbling a ball, passing, or rebounding. As an account leader, it could be reading people, connecting with others, being authentically vulnerable, and allowing others to feel the same freedom to be authentic and vulnerable themselves.

It could be giving gifts, being artistically talented and creative, funny, and lighthearted. Perhaps you're the person who keeps everyone on the same page and encourages others to do the same.

> AWARENESS ISN'T ARROGANCE; IT'S CLARITY. LEADERS WHO KNOW THEIR OWN BEST HELP OTHERS EXPRESS THEIRS.

Everyone has a unique gift, and to bring out the BEST in others is to home in on discovering it, spotlighting it, and utilizing it.

That's Enough

Basketball is played with five players on the court for each team. Additionally, most teams have three to seven players on the bench who rotate throughout the game. One extremely gifted and talented person cannot accomplish what five to twelve players can do when they're at their best. Whatever is your best is perfect. It's enough. That's enough! One player can't compete against five others at their BEST.

Your best is enough. Stop trying to be everything; be what you are.

In chapter 1, I noted that when members of the Impact Driven Leader Roundtable share their biggest insecurities, they overwhelmingly express fear of not being enough. For some reason, society, peers, parents, coaches, and leaders have convinced us our best isn't good enough. Some use this tactic thinking it motivates, drives humility, or puts people in their place. I think it's really their insecurity showing. They, too, don't feel they are enough, so they try to lower someone else to elevate themselves.

Outside of my office—well, my storage shed studio; let's not make it seem so glamorous—just beyond the fence around the pasture where my cows graze, stand hundreds of western white pine trees. These trees stretch over one hundred feet into the sky, providing shade for my cows and habitat for turkeys, deer, owls, and more. If harvested, these trees become construction materials, pulp for paper, matchsticks, and furniture. The desk where I'm writing this book is made of reclaimed wood from a building we once owned. It was once standing in a forest no different from the one on the other side of the window. The tree was perfectly made to become a piece of furniture. It was enough.

No one had to inject it with materials to make it stronger, but it did need refinement. A tree was cut down, milled, sanded, and perfected to become the desk.

The process the tree endured to become a piece of furniture and to live out its purpose happens to each of us. Our walls are the roughness that needs to be milled, refined, and sanded to help us accept that we are enough. It sometimes takes work to accept that you don't need to be someone else to have impact, it takes humility to bring out the best in us, and that's enough.

Accepting your strengths frees others to do the same. We bring out their best; we allow those in our circle to shine. To be what only they can be, and when we do that, we get to be what only we can be. And that's enough!

Serve

Basketball has ten players on the court and one ball. Winning requires all five teammates to contribute. Many teams fall apart when one or two try to dominate, which is why Coach Wooden focused on each player's best, and when they performed best together.

Work is the same. Create space, set others up, pass information, and elevate strengths. We're at our best when we serve others.

The NBA wasn't always a ratings story. For a stretch in the 1980s and 1990s, it was must-see television. Magic Johnson. Larry Bird. Then Michael Jordan. Different players, different styles—but all of them made basketball feel like it belonged to everyone watching.

Then something shifted.

The numbers tell part of the story. At its peak in 1998, the NBA Finals drew nearly 29 million viewers per game. By the 2020s, that number had fallen to roughly 11 million.[11]

More than fifty percent gone.

Nobody agrees on exactly why. Cord-cutting. Load management. Too many games. Players jumping teams before fans can attach.[12] There's no shortage of theories.

But one keeps coming up, even from legends inside the game. The product changed. Somewhere along the way, basketball became a one-or-two-man show. Players standing around while a star dribbles at the top of the key. And when that happens, fans feel it. The game is less fun to watch when only one person is playing it.[13]

Basketball is better when everyone's involved.

So is leadership.

In our modern workplaces, the parallel is stark. A recent Gallup poll found that 58 percent of workers are disengaged.[14] That's like three of the five players watching the game while on the court! Two engaged players can't compete against a team where all five contribute. To be at your best, you must serve others.

Timing

Timing is the last piece and the most important. You can have the gifts, accept that "that's enough," and want to serve, but if it happens at the wrong time, oh, boy, that can be disastrous. In basketball, if your team doesn't have the ball, your job is to defend the basket. You might be in your "sweet spot," but if you're on the wrong side of the court, then the time isn't the right moment to shoot. Right spot, wrong time.

A mentor of mine once wrote, "There's a time for everything." Bringing out the best in yourself and others means knowing what, how, where, and *when*.

The great psychologist Abraham Maslow's law of the instrument applies here: "I suppose it's tempting if the only tool you have is a hammer, to treat everything as if it were a nail."[15] When we ignore timing, we start hammering, whether that helps or not.

I've struggled with this many times, most often with words. More than once, a friend has said, "What you said wasn't wrong, but, nope, not the right time." When we pound a nail too soon, insecurity is driving, and we damage relationships that need care, not force.

So, how do you develop timing? Through experience, practice, and reflection. Coach Wooden helped his players and teams discern when and where to shoot; mentors can help you do the same. Sometimes timing is intuitive; often it's learned.

Strategy reinforces it. I pointed out earlier that, strategically, it might not be the right time to shoot in some basketball games. In many sports with a game clock, the winning team may choose to "run out the clock." That is to hold on to the ball, maintaining possession without attempting to score points. In basketball, you might run "Four Corners." In soccer, you "Take It to the Corner Flag." In football, it's the "Victory Formation." Sometimes the best play is holding the ball.

This can also apply to some relationship circumstances, knowing "when" to deploy someone's unique set of skills and abilities for maximum return for everyone. For me, it's knowing when to help people see "through the window"—in a safe, private, comfortable environment, not through a public confrontation.

When we focus on bringing out the best in others, we bring out the best in ourselves.

Exercise: BEST Alignment Game Plan

1. **Be** Aware—Name your unique gift.
2. That's **Enough**—Accept that it's enough!
3. **Serve**—Use your unique gift to elevate others.
4. **Timing**—Choose the right moment. When can you deploy gifts to serve? Again, if you need help with timing, ask.

Step 1—Write Out Your BEST

Be Aware—What is your unique gift? What do others admire most?

That's Enough—Declare it: "My best is enough."

Serve—Where can your gift help others win? If you're not sure, ask.

Timing—When will you use it? Seek counsel if timing is unclear.

Step 2—Choose Two People That You Work with and Two Friends

Identify their BEST. What are they uniquely gifted at? Tell them that is enough. Find, create, or identify places, opportunities, and situations where they can express their gifts.

When you find your sweet spot and use BEST—Be Aware, That's Enough, Serve, Timing—you create real impact. But "best" doesn't sustain itself. Next, we'll keep the windows clean: replace limiting beliefs, practice daily mindset hygiene, and protect the clarity that lets you and your team see each other—and hit the right shots.

CHAPTER 8

KEEPING THE WINDOWS CLEAN

f your inner critic spoke out loud, it might sound like this:

How did you even graduate from college? You are quite possibly the dumbest person I have ever met. There is no way you are going to make it in life.

I have never seen someone so uncoordinated and unathletic in my entire life. Why don't you quit already? It would make it easier on everyone else if we didn't have to put up with your ineptitude.

You're a slacker; you'll never amount to anything. Are you good at anything? Are you and your sister even related? If so, she got all the good genes, and you got none.

Why can't you do anything right? You'll never figure it out. No one will ever love you. You're always the problem. You'll never be able to do it—what's the point of trying? You always screw things up. You're a total failure.

Would you work for someone who talked to you this way? My guess is an emphatic *NO.* I wish I could say I've never seen a coach, boss, or parent speak like this—but it's not true. Recently, my daughter shared that her friend's coach berated them in front of the entire team with remarks like these. It's bad enough when a leader says such things; worse still when we say them to ourselves. I've definitely been guilty of that.

So why do we do it? Because we tend to believe the lies our insecurities tell us, and outside voices become inside beliefs. You wouldn't work for someone who talks to you like this, so why do we let that voice lead our lives? Unfortunately, we often think worse about ourselves than anyone else does. These are the smudges on the window, and we're going to clean them.

This often comes from an outside source: a parent, teacher, older sibling, school bully, or coach. I recently spoke with a best-selling author of more than a dozen books. He never thought he would be a writer. Why? Because his fourth-grade teacher told him he would never do something as "crazy" as write books. He was dyslexic and struggled to read. In his mid-sixties, he recounted it as if she had said it earlier that day. Outside words become inside walls, unless we learn to scrub the glass.

Rise Above

Thomas Edison is credited with holding more than a thousand US patents. But his mother's intervention at a critical moment mattered as much as his ingenuity. Nancy Edison refused to let a teacher's negative talk define her son when he was a young student.

According to popular legend, one morning, Mrs. Edison received a note from Thomas's teacher, which read, "Your son is addled [mentally ill], and we cannot let him attend our school anymore."[16] She took young Thomas aside, sat him down for a mother-son chat, and planted a seed, then fertilized and watered it. Instead of telling Thomas what the teacher had said, she exclaimed that Thomas was a genius, that the school was unable to educate him because they did not have the teachers, and that she would take over his education. She changed the course of humanity.

In that moment, Mrs. Edison refused to let a label become a destiny. She replaced a verdict with a calling, and the trajectory of her son's life changed. That is the power of words: They can wound, they can heal, and when believed, they can build a future.

Thomas was not pulled from school because his mother believed he was unfit to be taught. She believed the teacher was unfit to teach her son. Her belief that Thomas "was a genius" pushed back against any negative talk.

This is the seed of negative self-talk. What starts outside burrows inward, taking root, and becomes the sounding board for your thoughts and actions. Negative self-talk is the inner dialogue that tears you down, attacks you, and undermines you. It grows from fears and insecurities that amplify your worst experiences, thoughts, and feelings.

When the seed of negative self-talk grows into a deep-rooted, broad-branched tree, it drives people to think worse of themselves than anyone else does. To underscore this, Dr. Caroline Leaf—when joining me for a podcast to discuss her book *Cleaning Up Your Mental Mess*—described negative thoughts as toxins. Toxic mental thoughts, she noted, can have the same impact on our body as a virus. She explained it this way:

> So we all know about the COVID virus. We all know that the COVID virus produces a response in our immune system. What you may not have known, and this is why this is so significant, is that thoughts are as real as a virus. And this toxic thought is going to stimulate the same response in the brain as if you had a virus in your body, or a bacteria or whatever. Because this threatens survival. Our brain and body are not designed for toxic issues or unmanaged toxic things. They're not designed for toxicity of any sort. So whether it's bacteria, a virus, or a toxic thought from a toxic experience or a toxic habit or a toxic reaction.[17]

TRANSFORMATION DOESN'T START WITH DOING MORE. IT BEGINS WITH BELIEVING DIFFERENTLY.

Mrs. Edison kept the "virus" of harmful self-talk from taking root in her son's mind, and we are all the beneficiaries of her resolve. Now think about how reframing your own beliefs and mindsets could impact you. Transformation begins with what you believe.

Nancy Edison believed in her son, and that belief became Thomas's driving force. Belief works like that—it's your single greatest superpower. Belief in yourself can move you toward what once seemed impossible; belief in others can draw out what they never thought possible.

Fixed Versus Growth

Beliefs are the coin you drop into the pinball machine—lights flash, the game starts, and everything comes alive. That coin sets the loop: beliefs spark thoughts, thoughts drive actions, actions create results, and results reaffirm beliefs. In *Mindset: The New Psychology of Success*, Dr. Carol S. Dweck defines mindset as "the beliefs people have about the nature of intelligence and talent." Those beliefs—yours and others'—shape how you think and act, and experience either reinforces or rewrites what you believe.

Dr. Dweck argues that people have a fixed or growth mindset. A fixed mindset is the belief that whatever they are, they will be. They have adopted negative talk-based beliefs. People with a growth mindset believe that they and others can be taught, regardless of what others think of them; genius can be made.

> In a fixed mindset, students believe their basic abilities, their intelligence, and their talents are just fixed traits. In a growth mindset, students understand that their talents and abilities can be developed through effort, good teaching, and persistence.[18]

Mrs. Edison didn't hold the mindset that Thomas was fixed; she believed in his capacity to grow. Here are a few additional examples of people who choose not to believe the negative talk.

Real Historical Examples

1. Albert Einstein

- **What he was told:** His teachers said he was "slow," "mentally handicapped," and would "never amount to much."
- **Reality:** Went on to transform physics and win the Nobel Prize.
- **Mindset shift:** Curiosity over conformity.

2. Walt Disney

- **What he was told:** Fired from a newspaper job because he "lacked imagination and had no good ideas."
- **Reality:** Built one of the most creative empires in history.
- **Mindset shift:** Rejection does not equal identity.

3. Oprah Winfrey

- **What she was told:** A TV producer told her she was "unfit for television news" *and fired her.*
- **Reality:** Became one of the most influential media voices in the world.
- **Mindset shift:** Pain became purpose.

4. Michael Jordan

- **What he was told:** Cut from his high school basketball team; the coach said he wasn't good enough.
- **Reality:** Became arguably the greatest basketball player of all time.

- **Mindset shift:** Failure-fueled focus.

Pop Culture and Fictional Examples

5. Marty McFly—*Back to the Future*

- **Told:** "You're a slacker. No McFly ever amounted to anything."
- **Shift:** Refused to repeat his family's limiting story—proved otherwise.

6. Happy Gilmore—*Happy Gilmore*

- **Told:** "You're not good at hockey," "You don't belong here," "You're a disgrace."
- **Shift:** Channeled what made him different into his strength.

7. Rocky Balboa—*Rocky*

- **Told:** "You're just a bum from the neighborhood."
- **Shift:** Belief in his heart mattered more than anyone's approval.

8. Elsa—*Frozen*

- **Told (and told herself):** "Conceal, don't feel."
- **Shift:** Accepting who she truly was brought freedom and strength.

9. Harry Potter

- **Told:** "You're nothing but a boy who lived in a cupboard."
- **Shift:** Found identity and courage in purpose, not in people's opinions.

Everyday Human Examples

10. The Student

- Told by a teacher: "You're not college material."
- Belief forms: "I'm not smart."
- Action: Stops trying.
- Result: Confirms the belief—until someone believes differently.

11. The Employee

- Told by a boss: "You're not leadership material."
- Belief forms: "I'm not meant to lead."
- Action: Stays small, doesn't risk.
- Result: Self-fulfilling prophecy—unless belief changes.

12. The Child at Home

- Hears: "Why can't you be more like your sister?"
- Belief forms: "I'll never be enough."
- Action: Acts out or overperforms—always chasing a standard that moves.
- Result: Worth stays tied to comparison, not identity—until someone reflects back who they actually are.

13. The Young Athlete

- Told by a coach: "You're too small," "too slow," or "you don't have what it takes to play at the next level."
- Belief forms: "I'll never grow. I will never be valued. I'm worthless."
- Action: They stay after practice, study film, build discipline, and outwork more "talented" players. Over time, they earn their spot—not because of natural ability, but because of consistent effort and belief. They eventually grow.
- Result: Mindset shift. Effort over excuses. Natural talent can open the door—but belief and persistence keep it open. In many cases, we just need to give it time.

MSU

The facilitator wrote the letters *M*, *S*, and *U* in large black letters on the flip chart at the front of the room. Turning to the small group of us, he asked if anyone knew what MSU stood for. I was attending one of the first sales training sessions at the start of my dairy nutrition consulting career.

In the room were a handful of other new hires. Ever eager to fill a silence, I blurted, "Michigan State University."

Not the answer. A few strange looks followed; everyone in the room—except one other Midwesterner—was from California. Michigan State was as far off their radar as fresh fruits and vegetables from a Midwestern farmer's diet in the fall.

MSU: Making Stuff Up. Well, I was really off base, but wildly impacted as I write about it twenty-five years later, as I vividly recall the bold black letters written on the flip chart and the older bald gentleman who led the class. *MSU* is seared into my mind. Why? Because it happens all day, every day. People make stuff up. Our belief-fueled narratives—our thoughts, driven by beliefs—create full-length films about what could happen, what others think, and what their actions could, should, or might mean. As a friend once shared with me, our minds go wild, "reading between the lines," but the reality is that *nothing* is written there.

We tell ourselves stories we would never admit to people out loud because they prop up our beliefs. Sharing them would invite our mindset to be challenged, which could lead us to discover that the beliefs we have held, which drive everything about us, are false.

When we are trying to protect our inner selves and guard our insecurities, we fear not just rejection but the possibility of finding out we've been wrong!

The way forward is to exchange limiting beliefs for empowering ones—and create a new mindset.

What limiting beliefs do you have about yourself? Maybe like my friend Michael, whose teacher told him he would never be anything because he couldn't read in the fourth grade. Or like Edison's teacher, who thought he was "addled." I used to believe I didn't have worthwhile value to offer others. Sure, I have value, but it's not "worthwhile"; my limitations overshadowed my gift because I didn't see my strengths and uniqueness as valuable.

That changed when two mentors poured their belief into me. They saw something in me that I couldn't see when I looked in the mirror. They sat across the table from me, looked me in the eye, and said, "I believe in you." One was John Maxwell; the other, Mark Cole, now leading Maxwell Leadership. Their belief surrounded and encouraged me—and taught me to pass it on.

Exercise: Cleaning the Windows of Belief

Purpose: To identify the beliefs shaping your mindset and intentionally exchange them for empowering ones that lead to transformation.

Step 1—Look at Your Reflection

"Would you work for someone who tells you what you believe about yourself?"

Take a few moments to write out *what your current "boss" sounds like*—the voice in your head narrating your self-worth and capability.

- What do you often tell yourself when you fail or fall short?
- What do you say about yourself when no one's listening?
- Whose voice do those beliefs sound like—a parent, a coach, a peer, or your own?

Step 2—Identify the Smudges on Your Window

"We think worse about ourselves than anyone else thinks or believes about us."

List *three negative beliefs* you carry about yourself. These may be words once spoken *to* you—or words you've spoken *over* yourself.

Negative Belief	Who/What Shaped It?	How It Affects My Thinking
"I'm not smart enough to lead others."	A teacher's comment in high school	I hesitate to speak up in meetings.

Step 3—Replace the Bulb (Edison's Lesson)

Thomas Edison's teacher once told him he was "too stupid to learn anything." His mother told him he was *brilliant* and *destined to learn differently* instead of reinforcing that belief. That belief shaped the man who gave light to the world.

Who has spoken *light* into your life when you were in darkness? Write their name and what they said.

Person	What They Believed About You	How That Belief Changed You

Step 4—Break the Cycle

Beliefs → Thoughts → Actions → Results → Beliefs = Mindset

1. Draw this loop in your journal or workbook.
2. Then, fill in each blank for one area of your life you want to transform (career, relationships, health, faith, etc.).

Examples

- Belief: "I'm not a natural leader."
- Thought: "No one listens to me."
- Action: Avoid speaking up.
- Result: Team disengagement.
- Reinforced Belief: "See, I'm not leadership material."

Now, reframe it with an *empowering belief*:

- Belief: "My voice adds value."
- Thought: "My contribution can help."
- Action: Share ideas more confidently.
- Result: Greater trust and collaboration.
- Reinforced Belief: "I am a capable leader."

Step 5—Exchange Limiting for Empowering

List a limiting belief you have identified; exchange it for an empowering belief. Now, what action can you take to reinforce it?

Limiting Belief	Empowering Belief	First Action to Reinforce It
I'm not a natural leader.	I can lead myself.	Develop a daily routine to read a leadership book.

Step 6—Growth or Fixed?

Circle the column that fits your mindset today in most areas of life:

Fixed Mindset	Growth Mindset
I avoid challenges.	I embrace challenges.
I see feedback as criticism.	I see feedback as growth.

Fixed Mindset	Growth Mindset
I'm either good or not.	I can improve with effort.
Failure defines me.	Failure refines me.

Step 7—Keep the Windows Clean

Transformation doesn't start with doing more. It begins with believing differently.

Every morning for one week, repeat this reflection:

"I am not what I once believed.

"I am what I choose to believe today."

Then write one new belief you're practicing seeing through.

Belief is where all this work begins to move. You've cleaned the window, challenged the old narratives, and chosen growth over the fixed stories that used to run your life. Now it's time to drop the coin—to put that belief into play so thoughts ignite, actions follow, and results start rewriting what you know about yourself. Chapter 9 asks the simplest, hardest question: Do you believe?

DO YOU BELIEVE?

Jordan called the play. "Fire-right gun 91." He looked at me, smiled, and said, "You got this."

I ran to the right side of the formation and settled into my slot receiver position. With a clap, Jordan—a college quarterback himself and an NFL camp invitee—signaled the snap. I shot forward, took three steps, planted my right foot, turned to my left, and like butter on bread, the football hit my hands. I pulled the ball tight to my body with my left hand and accelerated as fast as my thirty-nine-year-old body could take me.

"You're fast," the defender called out, tossing the compliment my way as I jogged back to the rest of my team to celebrate our go-ahead touchdown.

"If you think I'm fast, you're slow," I shot back before the words had time to settle.

I'd just run fifty-five yards, and he had run most of it chasing me. In my entire life, I had never been told I was a fast runner. If the defender had been middle-aged like me, I might have understood. But he wasn't. Teammates said he played college football and was an all-league defensive back, at least fifteen years younger than me.

How could he think I was fast? I couldn't be fast. Growing up, I was mocked for being slow in nearly every athletic endeavor. One time, while preparing for middle school football, my dad was doing drills with my younger brother and me. My six-year-old brother was faster than me. During high school basketball, I was the slowest and shortest on the court.

As a high school senior playing soccer, I remember outrunning a few players one time. But it never made me feel fast—it just meant they were slower, or it seemed that way to me at the time. Yet, here I was twenty-some years later, outrunning a defender for a score.

For decades, I had accepted the lie, the theory, and the belief that I was slow and there was nothing I could do to change it. So, since I was convinced that I was slow because I had always been slow, the defender must be slow too. It's deductive logic, right?

Around this same time, I was transitioning from coaching my son's soccer team to helping other, more credentialed coaches. One of the coaches who had played professionally and with whom I had built a close relationship shared his belief that you were either fast or you weren't. He was quick, always had been, and made a career, collegiately and professionally, out of being fast. This was additional evidence for me that the ability to run fast and efficiently was indeed a trait you were born with or not.

The thought never even crossed my mind; is it possible, with years of weight lifting, explosive exercise training, and flexibility training, that I could have actually become "fast"?

No. Not possible. I was slow and would always be slow.

Speed Is Built

Around this same time, a young, fast wide receiver named Adam Thielen started making waves in the NFL. At six feet, two inches tall, and around two hundred pounds, Adam had the size—a long-armed, big-handed body type—to be a leading receiver in the league. And more importantly, he was fast!

In the NFL, if a player can run a forty-yard dash in less than four-and-a-half seconds, that is considered elite. Before he entered the league, Adam ran the forty-yard dash in 4.45 seconds—elite! But Adam had to develop that speed.

Despite being an all-conference and all-state player his senior year, Adam's collegiate offers were limited after graduating, not because of his ability, but because of his lack of speed. Going into that season, he ran the forty-yard dash in about 4.9 seconds, a far cry from the level of speed that would make him an NFL receiving record holder.

I learned about Adam's speed development from my friend Ryan Englebert, who had started training him in college at the University of Minnesota, Mankato (NCAA Division II). Their work took him from a slow high school receiver to an elite speed athlete.

After his junior season, Adam would drive ninety minutes several times a week to train with Ryan. He believed he could become an NFL receiver, even though no one knew his name. His ability to run routes and catch the football made him a star in college; the speed he built made him a pro in the NFL.

His talent, combined with elite speed, made him a perennial Top 100 player as ranked by his peers and the "unsung hero" of the 2016 Minnesota Vikings. Adam wasn't limited by a belief that he was slow. He chose to believe he could be fast, did the work, and his results reinforced that belief. He set his mind on becoming an elite speed receiver.

I believed I was slow because I had the mindset that I was slow. This same process works with our insecurities or first attempts at something new: If we accept the lie that we're fixed, we won't pursue the growth needed to accomplish anything new. The great tragedy is choosing to believe a narrative that doesn't serve us or others. We settle, instead of bringing out the best in ourselves by bringing out the best in others.

Why We Don't Trust Leaders

We all carry adopted beliefs about our skills and abilities—stories shaped by others' judgments and past experiences—that are false. For many, those false beliefs extend beyond speed or appearance to how we influence others: our capacity to lead. Over time, broken promises and abuses of power have tarnished the very idea of leadership, leaving many to assume leaders can't be trusted—a suspicion with roots in everything from Cold War propaganda to modern scandals.

John Maxwell faced this directly when speaking in Bucharest, Romania, in the early 2000s. The auditorium was filled with people eager to hear the American speak. There was a hum of anticipation in the crowd. Just before taking the stage to share his insights on leadership and why everyone can and should aspire to lead, his translator pulled him close and said, "I know you speak about leadership, Dr. Maxwell. I want to bring to your attention something about the people here in Romania. We don't trust leaders. Being a leader in Romania is not a noble aspiration. It is the position that takes from people."

Nothing like a pat on the back and encouragement before speaking to thousands; in not-so-many words, he essentially told John: "You're going to do great, slugger. Just to let you know, the last three batters were hit by pitches, the pitcher is throwing rockets, and there are no more ambulances available in the Tri-State area."

When the Berlin Wall fell in late 1989, it did little to change the sentiment about leaders. Inevitably, those just beyond the reach of the communist apparatus—abuse, dehumanization, manipulation—stepped into the new democratic order. Communism collapsed, but trust and psychological safety did not immediately return for the millions who had lived under it. It's easy to understand why. For decades, generations had known only distrust and control. There was no personal ownership, no upward mobility, no freedom of choice—leaders decided work, social life, and the terms of everyday living.

Authority without trust. So John did what he does: He got up on stage and named the elephant in the room. As he shared at the 2024 Impact Driven Leader Summit, he connected with people, recognized their experience, and empathized with them in a vulnerable way. He wasn't trying to take from them. He gave from the heart, and the audience responded in kind.

John displayed empathy, which is the action of engaging and working to build trust. I define empathy as putting your arm around someone and walking with them. That picture guides how I try to engage empathetically. To put your arms around someone, you first need trust and a connection. I tried this one time in high school without either and got punched in the ribs, which leads to the second requirement: vulnerability. Raising your arms and exposing your vital organs is a fitting symbol of vulnerability. Then, find a pace that works for both parties. As the apostle Paul wrote in his second letter to the Corinthians: "Do not be yoked together with unbelievers" (2 Corinthians 6:14).

The term *yoked* was a familiar image in the early first century: a wooden beam binding two oxen by the neck so they move as one.

The key, and why it is so relevant to me in this context, is that being empathetic requires acting in ways that benefit others. Connection lets us move in unison. If one ox is bigger, stronger, or faster than the other, the yoke's shear injures, chokes, or kills them both. If I put my arm around someone and drag them, they will resist; if they drag me, I will object. We have to be in step.

It's the same in a relay race: The outgoing and incoming runners must match pace so that, at the moment of exchange, the handoff happens cleanly, effectively, and efficiently at full stride.

Believing you can make a difference is the start of leading— starting with yourself. Reframing that mindset is like believing you can be fast enough to beat a defender for a touchdown, whether in the city recreational flag football league or the NFL. The trust a quarterback places in a receiver to deliver the ball is empathy in action: When the two are in sync, success follows.

EMPATHY IS THE ACT OF ENGAGING AND WORKING TO BUILD TRUST.

The Empathy Spectrum: Forming Trust

Trust cannot be built without empathy. As John experienced in Romania, both sides must understand one another's aims and seek mutual benefit. Our beliefs, experiences, and mindset shape both our empathy and how others experience it.

It's easy to write about trust or elite speed; actually doing it is hard. I never had formal training or assessments—just a few moments when people told me I was faster than I thought I believed. You might have experienced that too: Someone might have said, "Wow, you handled that much better than I expected" (that was said to me when one trainer at our gym, whom I referenced in chapter 2, chose to resign). Or the day you finally stood up for yourself after being used by someone, yet again.

These are healthy displays of empathy—the middle ground between empathy without boundaries and boundaries without empathy. I call this paradigm the Empathy Spectrum, a phrase coined by Rory Vaden during a personal coaching session in April 2019.

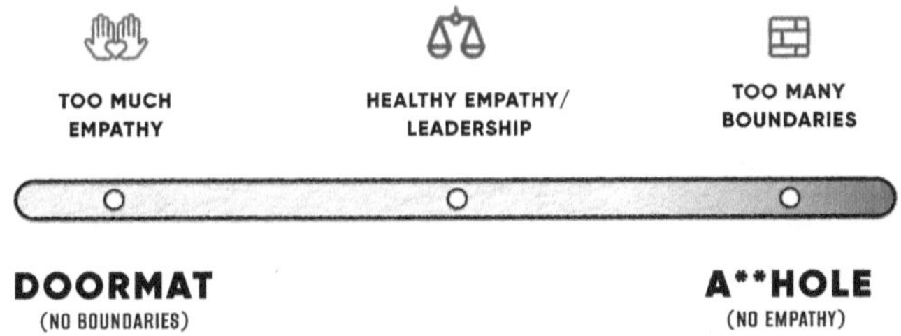

At one end is the Doormat.

They are inactive and isolated and let people walk all over them. They don't stand up for themselves. To feel valued, they keep giving in to others and avoid setting boundaries. They absorb others' emotions until they lose their own sense of self.

The other end, where I lived for years, is the A-hole.[19]

This person is hard-edged: emotionally distant, disconnected, intense and insensitive, focused on their own immediate needs and security. Often, like me, they are unaware that they are doing so. They are guarded and cold toward the people they lead. It becomes a mantra, a persona, or a modus operandi for leadership at its highest level.

Walking the Walk

Navigating the Empathy Spectrum is hard, which is why it requires reframing our mindsets and beliefs. If we cling to narratives and beliefs that feed our fears and insecurities, we struggle to open up, be vulnerable, and embrace boundaries and empathy. On one end, we must slow down to match others' pace and cadence. On the other hand, we must stand up for ourselves, even though it may upset others.

Healthy empathy is neither too soft nor too harsh—it's calibrated. But like developing speed, it takes time. It takes intentionality and consideration for others. Adam didn't go from moderate speed to elite speed in one training session. John didn't earn the Romanian audience's trust to transform their country in a single presentation.

They both had to walk the walk—practice over time—to move from each pole of the Empathy Spectrum to the middle, a healthy place where compassion and boundaries are in harmony.

To walk the walk is to walk with people, neither ahead nor behind. To be equally yoked is to see each other's value and maintain the proximity and connection needed to influence others. It starts with you: believing in yourself, accepting your value, and owning what you bring.

This can start with borrowed belief. This isn't "fake it until you make it." There is nothing more inauthentic than to be what you aren't. It is being your true self, the one others already see and believe in. We get there by opening our arms to others and letting them do the same. Insecurities that wall us off, or leave us as Doormats for others to rub their feet on, block that connection.

Next comes recognizing that our abilities aren't fixed—whether running, leading, influencing, or serving. We can grow into faster runners. We can become capable, empathetic, and trusted. We can lead others because leadership is needed, worthwhile, and noble. Leadership isn't a title or a role; it's the mindset that you can make a difference.

John Maxwell describes this as the leadership dance: sometimes you lead, sometimes you follow, sometimes you're side by side. Another key is that everyone is on the dance floor—no one watches from the balcony, detached from the action. Leaders stay engaged with everyone, regardless of position or title. They set the pace and rhythm as they listen to others' needs.

That's dancing—and that's leadership. When it happens, everyone has a place regardless of talent, ability, or title. Together, they build momentum, flow, and shared vision.

When everyone is engaged, dancing to the music, and finding their flow, empathy shows up in the dance as compassion and boundaries. It's the language of the heart—serving others to bring out their best.

Exercise: Empathy Spectrum Assessment

https://www.tylerdickerhoof.com/empathy

Below is an exercise to help you determine where you are on the Empathy Spectrum. This isn't and won't be static. In different situations and relationships, your indicator will shift. I encourage you to start with a personal relationship, then reassess with answers based on a work situation. Just as our insecurities show up differently across people and situations, our empathy oscillates and shifts with the circumstances.

Discover whether your empathy sits closer to the Doormat or A-hole end—or in the healthy leadership tension between them.

Instructions

Rate each statement on a scale of 1 to 5
(1 = Never true | 5 = Always true)

1. Empathy Without Boundaries (Doormat Tendencies)

1. I often feel emotionally drained after supporting others.
2. I struggle to say "no" even when I know I should.
3. I avoid conflict because I don't want to upset people.
4. I take on responsibility for other people's feelings.
5. I feel guilty when I set limits or prioritize my own needs.
6. I frequently compromise my standards to maintain peace.

→ High scores here = Empathy without boundaries (Doormat side)

2. Boundaries Without Empathy (A-hole Tendencies)

7. I tend to shut down emotionally when people share struggles.
8. I focus more on getting results than on how people feel.
9. I assume others should "toughen up" rather than need support.

10. I view vulnerability as a weakness in leadership.
11. I often give direct feedback without considering tone or timing.
12. I find it difficult to connect with people who disagree with me.

→ High scores here = Boundaries without empathy (A-hole side)

Scoring

- Doormat Total (Q1–6)
- A-hole Total (Q7–12)

Interpretation

- 18–30 (High) → You're living near that end of the Empathy Spectrum.
- 10–17 (Moderate) → You show tendencies but can recalibrate with awareness.
- 6–9 (Low) → You may lean too far toward the opposite pole.

Healthy Empathy Zone

When your two totals are within three to five points of each other, this reflects balanced empathy—compassion and boundaries—the tension where real leadership lives.

You've moved from belief to practice, calibrating empathy, earning trust, and leading in step. But this isn't a one-time shift; it's daily work. The focus now is simple and demanding: Know what you do best and keep sharpening it so your impact cuts clean. In chapter 10, we'll talk about how to stop being a drawer full of utensils and become the sharpest knife—choosing positivity, honing your edge, and using it to serve.

THE SHARPEST KNIFE

Got a question for you: Glass half full, glass half empty, or is there even a glass at all?

These three labels, often treated like fixed identities, have been used for generations to describe our outlook—positive or negative. They were popularized in the mid-twentieth century by psychologist Abraham Maslow and author Norman Vincent Peale, both of whom studied positive thinking.

Optimist, pessimist, and realist are the usual roles in the glass metaphor. You may have identified as one or the other, or others may have urged you to pick one of them. I've long considered myself a realist. Those close to me know what they're going to get.

Others have labeled me a pessimist. Those are people who fear the truth. Haha. Friendly banter, mostly. I have never thought of myself that way, but I have spent time around people who said things like, "we're broke," "when I win the lottery," "wouldn't it be nice," "that's just the way things go for me," "nothing good ever happens to me," and "the only thing I ever won was never winning." It can go on and on.

Only after I got away from those people did I realize how they had affected me. Unfortunately, many people in my life carried negative mindsets, and I didn't yet know I had the power to change my outlook—or my life.

After reading Jon Gordon's *The Power of Positive Leadership*, I realized I could change my outlook and choose to be more positive. Much of what I have written in this book has been influenced by Jon, who chose positivity despite a negative upbringing and mindset. Jon decided to be positive to improve—really, to save—his relationship with his wife, Kathryn, and his kids, Jade and Cole, and to show up better for everyone he met.

I often struggled to stay positive because I was wrestling with my fears and insecurities. Not feeling valued, worthwhile, or enough drove me to do more, be more, chase more. Whatever I did, I never felt like I was enough. That drive, while not self-centered, led others to believe everything was about me.

The intense desire, push, and work ethic didn't invite people into my life; it pushed them away, always making them feel as if whatever they did wasn't enough. I never felt great at anything. In my mind, nothing seemed to set me apart. I was good, but not great at anything—the classic "Swiss Army knife" of abilities.

The red-handled multitool was once a coveted gift and pocket tool. Born of necessity, like the development of my skill set working in agriculture, it outfitted the Swiss military with a tool that could open cans, service rifles, and handle general tasks. In 1891, Switzerland first purchased this tool from a German company before Swiss entrepreneur Karl Elsener began producing it at home.

This launched the company Victorinox, which has made the knives for over 130 years. While the tools are excellent for keeping everything you might need in your pocket, few people consider a Swiss Army knife the best knife, can opener, screwdriver, or corkscrew. I've owned a few: I was often disappointed because the scissors would break, the blade dulled quickly, the corkscrew snapped (not on a wine bottle), and most tools went unused. To this day, I would much rather carry one sharp-bladed knife for farm or outdoor chores.

To change how I saw my value, I had to let go of being a utility player, good at a lot of things, but not the go-to for anything.

My friend John Ruhlin, author of *Giftology* and master gift giver, taught me this lesson through a gift. As Cutco's all-time top knife salesperson, John discovered the power of being the go-to. Cutco, the direct-sales knife company, has a long and respected history of making high-quality, durable, sharp knives. Their tagline reads "Trusted in Kitchens Since 1949," and John delivered on that line.

As John explained to me, there's no substitute for the sharpest knife in the kitchen. You probably have one you reach for every time. For my wife, it's always the eight-inch bread knife for everything—bread, sure, block of cheese, of course, opening a package, why not—because it's her trusted go-to. I reach for the one that always seems sharp enough, no matter when it was last sharpened. And then, on super special occasions, there is one special knife, still in its box, with the cardboard sheath still on the blade. The blade itself is engraved with a message from John: "Handcrafted Exclusively for the Tyler and Kelley Dickerhoof Family." It is in the top-right drawer of our kitchen island.

It's special, and I know exactly when to use it. It has practical value—because it is amazingly sharp—and emotional value because when I use it, I think fondly of my friend. Here's the lesson: Be the sharpest knife in the kitchen, not just another utensil in the drawer.

You are a sharp knife. You have unique, distinct, and wonderful gifts that can impact people in remarkable ways. But if you're content being just another utensil in the drawer, you won't serve people in the most impactful way.

For me, there is a big difference between my go-to knife and the utensil drawer. Forks or spoons are interchangeable. They are not unique; they don't have a story, a box, or an engraving to signify them. If we choose to be just another utensil in the drawer, we rob ourselves and others of our true purpose. This is a choice, just like choosing to be positive.

One more way this lesson was driven home, and yes, at this point, I should probably just call this the "John" chapter, because this is a different John entirely: John Maxwell showed me how to take what I'd learned and turn it outward, using it to serve and lead others rather than staying locked in what I previously believed. He had to develop his own leadership. He wasn't always the best. Early in his career, some coworkers made a T-shirt that read, screen printed across the front: "It's hard to be humble when you're as great as I am."

Zing!

John had a choice: keep cutting with a dull knife, or seek help to sharpen it. He is the world's foremost expert in leadership today because he chose the latter. He didn't do it alone; he grew his capacity and calling to lead by example and show people the way.

He also learned that people want to follow someone who offers hope for a better, brighter future—someone with a vision who invites them into it. We can't do this by forcing people to join us, and we can't be all the utensils in the drawer. We have to be the sharpest knife in the kitchen.

One more lesson I learned from the Johns: Our greatest strength and our hope for better days are within our control. But we won't get there by trying to be what we aren't. As Jon Gordon models, no matter what challenges we face, the world can and will conspire for us. It is up to us to choose that mindset rather than letting our fears and insecurities tell us a false, destructive story about what we can't be; otherwise, we will settle.

We each have something we can be world-class at—often, it's a gift we don't even see as one. I have embraced being me. I have unique gifts that allow me to connect authentically, empathize with others, and encourage them. My gifts can become barriers (intensity) or binders (curiosity), depending on how I use them. The way forward is to focus on my strengths. It makes me stronger and the knife sharper. I will never be the most desired spoon in the kitchen, but I can be the sharpest, most meaningful knife. As John Maxwell teaches, taking an "eight-out-of-ten" ability to a nine- or ten-out-of-ten makes you world-class. But moving a three-out-of-ten to a five-out-of-ten leaves you average. A butter knife, even the best brand in the world, still isn't sharp enough.

Sharpen It Every Day

When my sons were younger, one of them fought taking showers—hardly uncommon. After long days of play, he was tired, and we were exhausted, so it was often a scrub fest before bed. We simply marked the task off the list. Once he was old enough to bathe himself, he learned to avoid it.

We could usually tell he skipped—not full-on egregious body odor, but that unmistakable dirty-kid smell. It's distinct. For me, growing up, skipping wasn't an option. Spend five minutes in a barn full of cows, manure, and everything else, and every part of you becomes drenched in the aroma. That's just being in the barn. Spend twelve to fourteen hours in it, and you start to go nose blind. Showers were a daily, sometimes twice-daily, requirement.

Mindset and beliefs work the same way: Reframing them is a daily practice, not a set-it-and-forget-it. Every day, multiple times a day, intentional action and discipline are required to avoid "smelling bad." The soap we use to clean our mindset is belief. As I mentioned in chapter 8, *Mindset* is *Beliefs* that drive *Thoughts*, leading to *Actions*, then *Results*, which in turn reinforce *Beliefs*.

Belief as a cleanser can start within, but it also comes from others. When self-belief combines with others' belief in us, our value compounds.

THE CIRCLE OF OWNERSHIP

Our greatest value is the expression of a mindset dedicated to making a lasting impact on others. It was this revelation that drove me to embrace being an Impact Driven Leader and to help others do the same.

An Impact Driven Leader is one who, despite vulnerabilities, shortcomings, and mistakes, future and past, pursues a vision of a better tomorrow through influence and partnership with others. My mission is to help other leaders do the same: authentically embrace their vulnerabilities in the service of others. It gives me purpose—and it gives meaning to my brother Joel's life.

A key distinction is understanding the difference between chasing success and finding significance. As John Maxwell writes, "Success is about us. Significance is about others."[20] To be the sharpest knife in the kitchen means going all in on what only you can do—abandoning the idea that value comes from being good at everything, and instead choosing to be great at what's uniquely yours. This varies for everyone, which is why comparisons fail.

In corporations and on sports teams, spots are limited; a person can be cast aside in one place and thrive in another. In one kitchen, you're a dull knife; in another, razor-sharp. The driver is belief—belief in yourself, and belief from others.

Your Impact Vision

In *The Vision Driven Leader,* Michael Hyatt describes vision as "a compelling vision as one that is clear, inspiring, practical, and attractive—a picture of your organization's future that your team can rally around and make real."[21]

When you have a vision for how to use your unique gifts—your sharpest knife—you always find ways to impact others. This may come through a "leadership title" or simply through influence. When I felt lost, not sure who I was, how I could serve and impact others, or even how to provide for my family, I lacked a vision for how I could impact others.

Impacting others is not about building wealth, climbing the corporate ladder, or winning awards. Those may come, I've seen it firsthand, but chasing success won't lead to significance, and significance is impact. Significance quiets fears and insecurities.

A vision is a picture of hope. A vision is not a one-man band; it's an invitation for others to harmonize in the symphony. My vision can coexist with and surround yours, without diminishing or overshadowing it. I'm only one person, one knife, one set of gifts; you bring a different blade. A leader committed to impacting others recognizes that the best full-length movies are ensembles—a collection of scenes, characters, challenges, and triumphs—created together.

Anyone can—and should—create an Impact Vision.

Imagine I pick you up and we drive to your favorite restaurant so we can eat together, ask questions, learn about each other, laugh, and share an experience. I couldn't do it without knowing how to get to the restaurant, right? Without directions or a destination, we're going nowhere. At some point, I need the restaurant's name or address.

Vision works the same way.

We could still have a lovely evening and enjoy the drive, but without a destination, you would eventually want to get out. This happens all the time in our lives: We take jobs because the invitation seemed appealing, hop in for a ride, then ask, "Where are we going?" Or we enter a relationship planning to figure it out on the way—the adventurous, free-for-all type—until one person wants Italian and the other South Asian—different destinations.

What started as a clear, inspiring, practical, planned, and future-oriented vision turned into a nightmare. Without a shared vision, razor-sharp skills get treated like a cheap, dollar-store multitool. What was once hopeful and inspiring turns into despair, finger-pointing, blame, missed opportunities, and hurt. Layer in negative thoughts, fear, and insecurity, and you've stepped into many a broken C-suite office—where personal survival is the king.

An Impact Vision honestly acknowledges one's limitations and strengths, past and future, and paints a clear, inspiring picture in which one's most significant impact is realized by growing, empowering, and elevating others.

A person with an Impact Vision will lead others. Without it, a leader just drives until their car breaks down. Let's work together to find you a destination worthy of a multi-Michelin-star meal that Will Guidara would be proud to serve.

Before we get there, let me tell you about my friend, Will Guidara. I learned about him several years ago, when his book, *Unreasonable Hospitality*, became a bestseller. What drew me to Will was his heart and his compassion for serving and seeing others—using what he's great at. Fun fact: Will and I spent four years at the same school in the same city without ever meeting!

Will has become one of the most influential voices in modern hospitality and leadership. Best known as the former co-owner and general manager of Eleven Madison Park, he helped transform a struggling New York restaurant into one of the most celebrated dining experiences on the planet—earning three Michelin stars and the title of the World's Number One Restaurant.

Will's leadership wasn't built on ego, bravado, or perfection. It was built on something profoundly human: the belief that people feel valued when leaders go above and beyond to create meaningful experiences. This is the heart of his philosophy, which he calls Unreasonable Hospitality—the idea that extraordinary impact comes from seeing people deeply and serving them generously.

He didn't set out to run the best restaurant in the world; he set out to create the most unforgettable experiences in the world. That was his Impact Vision—using his sharpest knife. He owned his past, his failures, and his doubts, chose to build something bigger than himself, and multiplied his impact through partnership, empowering his team, and elevating others. He pursued a future that didn't exist yet—and brought others with him. That's the essence of an Impact Vision.

When I say, "Let's work together to find you a destination worthy of a multi-Michelin-star meal that Will Guidara would be proud to serve," I'm not talking about food.

I'm talking about the level of intentionality, excellence, and people-centered impact that Will models. Your Impact Vision is the menu you write; your leadership is the service you offer; the impact you leave is the experience others carry with them. Will reminds us of this truth: You don't need a restaurant to serve people—you need a vision that elevates them.[22]

A vision that leaves a legacy. A vision bigger than you. A vision that sharpens you—and elevates others.

Before you can lead others to a better, brighter future, you must first believe that future is possible; and belief sets the mindset. We've learned through Jon Gordon's example that positivity is not naive—it's a *choice* that reshapes your life. We've learned through John Ruhlin that value comes from being the sharpest knife, not every utensil. We've learned through John Maxwell that leaders aren't born sharp—they become sharp through humility, awareness, practice, and community. And we've learned through Will Guidara that impact is created through intentional, excellent, people-centered service.

Now, you shape that learning into your Impact Vision—a clear, inspiring, practical, written picture of where you are going and why it matters.

Exercise: Create Your Impact Vision

Purpose: Write a clear, inspiring, practical picture of your future—where you're going and why it matters—so you can lead with significance.

How to use: Set a timer for 30–45 minutes. Write short, concrete answers. When done, draft a single-sentence vision.

Step 1—Your Mindset: From Glass to Gift

1. Historically, have you seen the "glass" as an optimist, pessimist, or realist?
2. Whose voices shaped that view?

My mindset has been shaped by the following:

____

____

3. What negative beliefs, comments, or environments shaped your self-story?
    Think of the "we're broke," "nothing good happens for me," "that's just how life is" voices.

Negative narratives that lingered:

____

____

4. What new beliefs will you choose moving forward?

Beliefs that sharpen you, not dull you.

____

____

Step 2—Your Knife: What Makes You Sharp

5. What is the one unique gift, skill, or presence that makes you
   a "sharp knife," not a Swiss Army knife?

My sharpest edge is the following:

____

____

6. Where and when does this sharp edge show up strongest?

____

____

7. How does this gift elevate or empower others?
         Impact is significance, not success.

My gift serves others by doing the following:

____

____

Step 3—Belief: The Great Cleanser

Mindset must be cleaned daily—like a shower. Belief is the soap. Belief in yourself + Belief from others = Your greatest value.

8. Who believes in you? List three names and what they see that you often overlook.

    1. _____________ believes I _____________________________.

    2. _____________ believes I _____________________________.

    3. _____________ believes I _____________________________.

9. How will you daily "shower" your mindset? What two to three intentional habits will reinforce belief (e.g., morning reflection, outreach, practice)?

My daily belief rituals:

____

____

____

Step 4—Creating a Picture of Hope

Michael Hyatt defines vision as "a clear, inspiring, practical, and attractive picture of your organization's future."[23] Your Impact Vision is not a fantasy. It is a destination. A place you can name, articulate, and invite others into—like giving someone directions to their favorite restaurant.

10. Describe your picture of a better future—your future self, sharp, focused, and fully utilized.

My picture of hope:

____

____

11. Who will be impacted by that future?

My vision will elevate the following:

____

____

12. What makes this vision bigger than you? How does it create significance, not just success?

My vision is bigger than me because of the following:

____

____

Step 5—Your Impact Vision Statement

Now combine everything into one sentence:

- Your unique gift
- Your sharpened mindset
- Your belief
- Your purpose
- Your commitment to significance
- Your desire to elevate others

Pick a template and fill it, if helpful:

Template A—Simple and Strong

"I will use my gift of ___________ to create ___________ so that ___________ can experience a better future."

Template B—Knife Metaphor

"I will be the sharpest knife in the kitchen by ___________, serving others through ___________, so that the impact of my life is felt through the growth and elevation of those I lead and love."

Example—Impact Driven Leader

"Despite my vulnerabilities and imperfections, I choose to press toward a future where my unique gifts create significance by empowering, elevating, and partnering with others."

Now write yours:

My Impact Vision Statement

____

____

____

____

____

Step 6—The Guidara Standard
Will Guidara showed the world that impact is created when leaders choose excellence, intentionality, and a relentless commitment to elevating others.

13. How will your vision reflect Unreasonable Hospitality? How will you serve, see, and elevate people the way Will did—no restaurant required?

I will embody unreasonable hospitality by doing the following:

____

____

Step 7—Final Step: Set Your Destination
Just like planning a dinner with a friend, your future requires a destination. You are now setting yours.

14. Name the destination of your Impact Vision (specific outcome in twelve to twenty-four months). If someone rode with you, would they know where you're heading?

- Three actions you'll take this month
- One metric you'll track weekly
- Review cadence (e.g., Friday fifteen-minute check-in)

The destination I'm driving toward is

____

____

____

You're ready: You now have a clear, inspiring, practical written picture of your future—where you're going and why it matters— built to be acted on and shared.

CHAPTER 11

LINK ARMS TO SURVIVE THE SURF

It was cold and wet. The air hung heavy with ocean humidity. A dense marine layer of fog stretched as far as the eye could see along the peninsular coastline.

The morning sun was just creeping in, rising ever so slightly over San Diego Bay.

To the north, distant dark figures were moving in an orderly fashion. Their diligence was unmistakable—like ants gathering provisions, they never missed a beat.

This was Coronado, a peninsula in Southern California, just west of San Diego. My wife and I were visiting, and this was the scene that lay before me as I had gotten up early to go for a run. OK, I'm not sure if I've emphasized this yet, but I'm not a runner—really, it's more that running doesn't suit me.

Give me a game, a sport, a reason, and I'll run for hours if needed. Yet I have never had a desire to compete in triathlons or run marathons; I don't even run 5Ks. The longest I have ever run is a 7K. Personally, I don't see the point. While some people find solace in running, for me, running is mostly pain—especially in my right shoulder. A knot grabs the middle of my right trapezius muscle and tightens like a vice, feeling worse than being impaled with a sharp object. Unfortunately, I know that kind of pain, but "three inches from bleeding out in college" is a story for another book!

When I do run outside of a sport, it's for my overall health. I would rather unload a couple of tons of hay to feed my cattle. I'd rather work for hours landscaping, fixing fences, building something, knee deep in mud, manure, or water. Anything but running.

But here I was, jogging from the Hotel del Coronado toward the Naval Amphibious Base along Coronado Beach—the place that hosts, tests, and certifies SEAL candidates. As I inched closer to the base, I could see them working together to complete the tests, drills, and exercises.

Several years later, I became friends with a few operators who served as SEAL commanders at the highest levels of rigor. Their stories have impacted me most, not for the immense sacrifice and physical demands required to complete Basic Underwater Demolition/SEAL (BUD/S) training, but for what it takes to survive the grueling testing. Coronado is only a small segment of a nearly two-year process. The initial portion is in the Great Lakes. As a guy from Ohio, I can see why San Diego would feel like a delight after two months on Lake Michigan, at least at first.

To qualify for Coronado, candidates must first prove their individual fitness. But everything changes in the Pacific Ocean theater. This is what I asked my friends, whom I'll call Pete and Owen: "How do people survive BUD/S training?" Without hesitation, Owen said, "That's easy!"

Well, OK then, let's get to it.

Before I share his answer, let me give you some context: For every person who earns their SEAL Trident, the reward for passing all the stages of the SEAL candidate process, there are between fifty and one hundred who have attempted it.[24] The words Pete and Owen shared with me carry tremendous weight. They each led at the highest level in the US Navy. Each served long and illustrious careers as SEAL Team commanders and trainers.

Owen said, "That's easy," as if he'd cracked the code. His answer didn't make me think I couldn't make it; it showed me I wouldn't make it as the person I thought I had to be to survive. As a Midwestern farm kid routinely logging fourteen-plus-hour days in conditions that make San Diego feel mild, I realized I could have survived. In truth, I had already survived worse.

Try feeding cows, breaking ice six inches thick, fighting rain and wind that blows you sideways, while covered in manure, mud, and sweat. Wrestle hay bales that weigh half your body weight for hours in hot, humid conditions, then milk and feed the same animals before dawn and after dusk. Shoot, playing in a salty, wet sandbox sounds like a vacation day.

Link Arms

Owen's answer to the question, "How do people survive BUD/S?" was simple: Don't try to do it alone. You are stronger when you link arms with the people beside you. Move past the self-sufficiency mindset and adopt a collective, empathetic mindset.

Pete interjects. For him, "linking arms" to survive takes a twist as he recounts being on a mountain ridge in the Middle East. As the commanding officer, he was responsible for getting his team home to their families. They were awaiting a helicopter exfiltration after an unnamed mission—details were need-to-know. The mission isn't the main character in this particular story; what the other SEALs did for each other is.

Weather delayed the exfiltration, so they settled into a defensible position on the ridge. What was supposed to be a California-style stop for burgers, fries, and a chocolate shake, a.k.a. a quick In-N-Out, became more of a sit-down banquet, and none of the squad wanted to be the main course.

"Cap, you good?" crackled through the earpieces, checking that Pete had what he needed.

Pete responded, "Yeah, I'm good." Then a barrage of check-ins rolled through the team, with everyone confirming readiness.

"I got plenty of water. Does anyone need some?"

"I'm low on ammo."

"I got you, got an extra clip coming your way."

Pete said this went on for a few minutes, until each member was positioned to defend themselves against the surrounding enemy. They waited for twelve hours like this. All arm in arm, linked to survive. It's the only way, as they had all learned years earlier on the beach, getting pounded by the cold, salty, unrelenting Pacific Ocean waves.

The person who tries to do it on their own loses. In the surf, on the ridge, in the boardroom, weight room, or any room. It doesn't matter where you are; if you try to do it all on your own, you will not survive.

Now, let me put a dash of seasoning on this concept. There are exceptions: people who survive on their own. Some "conquer" BUD/S training by sheer will through tremendous physical, emotional, and technical strain. But as I learned, just because you make it through the candidate process and receive your Trident, it doesn't guarantee you will ever be selected to serve arm in arm with others. Some people make it all the way through and still don't end up with a career as an operator. They may have willed themselves to the finish line on their own, but they missed the skill BUD/S is designed to teach: We are stronger together.

We go it alone out of fear and insecurity. Those stories convince us that the only way to survive is to put up and maintain walls—to protect our vital organs by keeping our arms tight to our chests. The stories fear tells us are not about being vulnerable; they are about protecting ourselves at all costs. SEAL candidates must overcome that. By linking arms, they embrace vulnerability and become stronger. They make their growth about others to help silence the stories of fear. The vulnerability of linking arms gives strength. Offering water, provisions, or ammunition may seem to leave individuals exposed, but it strengthens the entire squad and increases everyone's chances of survival.

A candidate who is stuck in the mindset that survival is purely personal becomes a liability to themselves and everyone around them. This is not unique to SEAL candidates; you see the same principle in every preflight safety presentation. The attendant stands in the aisle, positioned throughout the cabin, showing the location of the exits and how to operate the seat belts, flotation devices, and oxygen masks. No doubt, each of these items is being demonstrated because, at some point, people instinctively understood that passengers would behave differently. The instructions to "put your oxygen mask on yourself before helping others" seem inconsequential to a solo traveler and counterintuitive to a parent of young children. It's counterintuitive in BUD/S too: To survive, they must help the candidate beside them compete.

That counterintuitive move improves your odds of survival. Linking arms with others builds strength and resolve. Putting on your oxygen mask first ensures your lungs receive the air they need to sustain you, so you stay conscious and can help others.

Recognizing our fears and insecurities, owning how they show up, and reframing our mindset and beliefs—that's life's oxygen mask. It's about understanding that the way to survive isn't about competing with others; it's about combining strengths to create survival and significance. I learned from reading Simon Sinek's book *Together Is Better*, we are not meant to do it alone.

As I've adopted: *We have to do the work on our own, but we don't have to do it alone.* This is what fuels growth: doing it for others. Learning how to link arms and putting on your oxygen mask first requires growth: authentic vulnerability, clear awareness of your abilities, appreciation of others' gifts and abilities, and the humility to strengthen each other. Recognizing strengths mutes the inner stories that feed fear and insecurity. When we choose to grow intentionally in service of others, strengthening our capacity to support them, our fears and insecurities lose their hold.

Going back to the John Maxwell quote from the last chapter: "Success is about us. Significance is about others." That's the foundation of an Impact Vision, and it requires others. John Maxwell has long taught that the bigger the dream, the more you need other people. Dreams that outgrow you can't be accomplished alone.[25] To link arms, we need to *grow.*

The last piece of reframing your mindset is believing you can lead. That belief frees you to focus on the growth needed to be the leader others need! Start by believing in yourself *first*—put your fears and insecurities in their place.

Awaken → Grow → Lead

This is the Impact Driven Leader framework. Through this book, we have covered Awaken—recognize your fears and insecurities, own how they show up, and reframe your mindsets and beliefs. The next phase is to Grow—first for yourself, then for others, and finally with others. Last, Lead—clarify a vision, connect with others, and earn influence. Together, these create Impact!

Before I leave you, I want to share a way to continue awakening each and every day. It's a process I call the Five R's of Mindset. It is a simple practice that helps you reframe your mindset and beliefs.

The **Five R's of Mindset** are more than a strategy; they are a daily journey into your identity. They shape how you show up, how you lead, and how you grow:

- **Routine**—the architect of excellence
- **Remember (or Not)**—the vault of victories
- **Rest/Reset**—the sanctuary of strength
- **Realistic**—the mirror of truth
- **Repeat**—the rhythm of progress

Routine

Routine is the architect of excellence, because we don't just end up where we want to go by accident. We set a destination in our maps application, plot the route on a trail map, or focus on the practices that will sharpen our knife. A routine creates freedom because we can only make so many decisions each day, and constant choice-making can push us off course. Decision fatigue crushes our mindset: It erodes beliefs, thoughts, actions, and results.

Some people thrive on routine; others loathe routines. Either way, everyone has one. Build yours with intention. Maybe you wake at a set time every day like I do, or maybe you wake up whenever you wake up. Both are routines. What do you do next? That's routine too. It's not bad; it's simply you. Instead of assuming you can't dictate your day, decide where you want to go and chart the course.

In my twenties, I worked out in the early evening. Now, I enjoy working out in the morning because it would be much harder in the evening, given the demands of my family and businesses. Circumstances change, and so can your routine. I have a morning routine focused on supporting my mind and body in being their best. Mine now starts with water, supplements that support my body's performance, and time for reading and journaling.

Remember (or Not)

When my kids were younger, we watched *Finding Nemo* on repeat. Partly because we all liked it, and partly because the movie was always in the DVD player, so it was easy to just press play. It was the days of DVDs and Blu-rays. (Wow, those hit the early 2000s bingo card for this book.) Actually, that sounds like a lot of fun. Create bingo cards for random cultural mentions in books. If you like the idea and create a thriving business, just give me a shout-out; there's no need for royalties. Dory, one of the movie's key characters, has short-term memory loss. While this makes certain aspects of her life challenging, such as meeting new acquaintances again, it also keeps her from harboring negative thoughts.

Reflecting on our days—our thoughts, experiences, wins, and setbacks—is essential. But we don't have to remember everything. If it doesn't serve you, do what Ted Lasso instructed his players: Have the memory of a goldfish!

Rest/Reset

Moving from remember (or not) to reset means knowing when to walk away. When I first moved to California after college, I lived with a longtime friend from my days of competing in dairy knowledge bowl contests. As I mentioned in chapter 3, he was working on a dairy farm and had an extra room in the house he was provided. The person who helped him get the job lived a mile away on his own farm, and we often went to his house to help, have dinner, and hang out. Only a few years older, he was very much like a big brother to both of us.

"Just shut it down and walk away, all you're going to do is make it worse," George told us one afternoon. For a couple of guys who had never even thought of this, the idea was revolutionary. You mean, in the middle of trying to dig a tractor out of the mud, or dealing with a highly fraught and angry cow, you can just walk away? Wow! I had never heard such a thing. Here is a way you can apply it: In a tough moment, shut the laptop, close your eyes, lean back in your chair, and reset. The perspective you can gain by stepping away and returning with a clearer, calmer mind is remarkable. This isn't quitting or walking away and forgetting it; it's pressing reset so you can come back energized and ready to address the problem with a fresh perspective. Control what you can, and let go of what you can't. Build daily resets into your routine.

Realistic

In *Good to Great*, Jim Collins writes about the Stockdale paradox. Simply put, the POWs who survived the longest under the North Vietnamese were those with a realistic view of their circumstances. The optimists struggled the most because they simply didn't have the mindset to endure; the pessimists lost heart. Rather, it was the realists who survived; they had unwavering faith that they would not just survive, but prevail as a great company. And yet, at the same time, they became relentlessly disciplined at confronting the most brutal facts of their current reality.[26]

Face the facts regarding your fears and insecurities. It isn't a one-time event. Our fears and insecurities are with us for life, so realistically address them daily.

Repeat

Like brushing our teeth or bathing, if we don't tend our mindset daily following the Five R's, we will start to stink. I don't get it perfect every day, but I know where I will be at 5:00 a.m. on Monday: waking up, drinking water, reading Proverbs, and doing something to grow where I need it. It's been well over eight years—every day, no matter where I am.

Now, let's walk through it together.

Exercise: The Five R's of Mindset

Purpose: A guided practice to shape your mindset, sharpen your leadership, and strengthen your daily rhythm.

1. Routine—"The Architect of Excellence"

A routine doesn't restrict you—it frees you. People without patterns live in constant tension. People with rhythm move with clarity.

Reflection Questions

1. What parts of your day already have structure?
2. What areas of your life feel chaotic or unpredictable?

3. Which habits (phone, nutrition, fitness, growth, humility, reading/journaling) do you want to build into your routine?

Action Step

List your ideal daily script—the routine that sets you up to lead.

Morning Routine

____

Workday Routine

____

Evening Routine

____

2. Remember (or Not)—"The Memory That Serves You"

Like Dory in *Finding Nemo*, sometimes the healthiest thing is forgetting what no longer needs space in your mind. Like Ted Lasso says, "Be a goldfish."

Reflection Questions

1. What past moments do you replay that drain your confidence?
2. What victories have you forgotten to celebrate?
3. What is one negative memory you need to release?

4. What truth or lesson do you want to *remember* instead?

Action Step
Write down one thing you're letting go of, and one you're holding on to:

Letting go: ____

Holding on: ____

3. Reset—"The System for Coming Back Strong"
Reset comes from

- routines;
- clarity of what you can and cannot control;
- serving others; or
- shutting it down when your mind and body need stillness.

Reflection Questions

1. What signals tell you it's time to reset?
2. What drains you the most in daily life?
3. What restores you the fastest?
4. Where do you need to accept that you are not in control?

Action Step
Design your Daily Reset Plan:

When I need to reset, I will:

____

____

4. Realistic—"The Mirror of Truth"

The Stockdale paradox teaches this essential leadership truth: "Never confuse faith that you will prevail in the end with the discipline to confront the most brutal facts of your current reality."

Leaders who tell the truth are trusted. Leaders who ignore the truth break trust.

Reflection Questions

1. What brutal facts about your current reality do you need to confront?
2. Where do you need to bring clarity, even if certainty isn't possible?
3. What truth do you need to say—to yourself or to someone else?

Action Step

Write the most honest sentence you can about your current situation:

____

Then write the hopeful sentence that pairs with it:

____

____

5. Repeat—"The Rhythm of Progress"

Mindset is not a set-it-and-forget-it system. It's more like bathing—you have to do it daily, or you will start to stink. Leadership is built in repetition.

Reflection Questions

1. Which of the Five R's do you most often skip?
2. What daily mindset practice do you need to recommit to?
3. What is one small action you can repeat every day for the next seven days?

Action Step
My Daily Repetition Commitment (Seven Days)

____

____

EPILOGUE

On my right arm, between the crook of my elbow and the start of my shoulder, covering the bicep are two scars from the same incident. One scar is the size of an Oreo, the other a deck of cards. I don't remember pouring boiling water on myself and suffering third-degree burns, but the evidence remains: rippling skin with raised edges that become raw and irritate faster than normal skin. Most days, I forget they're there. When I was younger, people would ask how it happened; now I can't even tell you the last time someone did.

When I was two and a half years old, I poured water from a tea kettle onto my arm and legs as my mother pulled me away from climbing onto the stove. She quickly poured cold water on my legs, limiting the damage. There are no scars from burns there. She has told me she didn't see the water soaking into my shirt on my arm—and that's why the scars remain.

The funny thing about scars, external and internal, is that they leave damage we may recognize or forget. Some scars we cover and hide; others we embrace as badges of resilience. How we internalize scars is very personal. I am essentially blind to the scar on my arm. Even when people point it out, I am caught by surprise. For some, they think the memory of the pain that formed it or the healing process should be seared into my mind. This quickly subsides when I tell them how young I was at the time.

My brother Joel also had a burn scar on his right forearm that only a few people would remember or know about. Even when scars fade, they can have a lasting impact on others.

External wounds leave external scars; internal wounds leave internal ones. External wounds can also create internal scars. Our fears and insecurities are the marks of internal wounds. In some cases, we know precisely when, how, and where they developed; the words, the situations, or the people involved. In other cases, we have no idea; we only feel their presence. Even if my mom hadn't told me what happened to my arm, the damage would still exist, and I'd still have to account for it, because it is part of me and always will be. Even if I tattoo over my scar or graft new skin, I would still have a scar and its story from the incident.

The goal isn't to erase scars; they shape who we are. With authenticity and vulnerability, we can let them speak, turning pain into purpose.

I boldly accept that my life could have been vastly different had the circumstances surrounding my brother's death been different. If it had not been deemed an accident, I could have faced some very serious consequences. Or if my parents had handled it another way, the last thirty-two years of my life would have been different. Still, I have chosen to give my brother's life purpose by doing the work to recognize how my scars impacted others. I was willing to heal the wounds of how I dealt with my fears and insecurities and speak from the scars.

I know you can do the same. Regardless of the wound, there is the ability to heal and develop a scar from which you can speak. Our speech in this world is impactful; impact becomes significance, and when we choose significance, we help give others' lives purpose.

Let's *grow* together by putting some windows into your walls.

ACKNOWLEDGMENTS

Whenever I read the acknowledgments at the end of a book, I always think, *Hmm, how did they not forget anyone?*

This list won't be exhaustive, but I would be remiss not to make this statement. I wouldn't have accomplished this feat without some very key people in the book-writing process.

First, to the late John Ruhlin, who referred me to Brand Builders Group to work with Rory Vaden.

Rory, for helping me discover that the main problem I aim to solve for people is insecurity. The Empathy Spectrum shed light on much of the content.

To Elyse Archer, who helped me in the very first elements, setting a foundation.

To Adam Flores for helping me discover the book's framework.

To Jeremy Weber, who helped me put up the walls and a roof.

To Taylor Spradling, who helped me fill the walls with insulation and install the utilities.

To Larissa Salazar for the final touches, the "chef's kiss."

Each of you helped construct what is in these pages.

The Streamline team, all of you, thank you for making the experience enjoyable and life-giving.

Jesse Pierpoint, thank you for displaying your genius and creating another masterpiece.

To Wednesday Consulting, there isn't enough I can say about the impact you have made.

And the cows—I wouldn't know what I know about leading people if I hadn't taken the time to learn from cows!

ABOUT THE AUTHOR

Tyler Dickerhoof is a leadership mentor, entrepreneur, and host of the *Impact Driven Leader* podcast. With over twenty-five years of experience and more than $700 million in generated business sales, he understands the real pressures leaders face.

A Cornell University graduate, Tyler once defined his worth by achievement, often at the expense of relationships. Through personal development and entrepreneurship, he confronted the hidden insecurities shaping his leadership. Today, he helps leaders slow down, tell the truth about what's really driving them, and lead with greater authenticity, clarity, and impact.

Tyler and his wife, Kelley, have been married for twenty years and live in Spokane, Washington, with their three children, Brittan, Braxton, and Landon Dickerhoof.

NOTES

1   Name changed for his protection, obviously, right? OK great, let's keep going.

2   Tyler Dickerhoof, host. 2021. *The Tyler Dickerhoof Show*, episode 9, "How to Clean Up Your Mental Mess with Dr. Caroline Leaf," March 12, https://podcasts.apple.com/us/podcast/ep-9-how-to-clean-up-your-mental-mess-with-dr-caroline-leaf/id1545349296?i=1000512664873.

3   Maurice Switzer, *Mrs. Goose, Her Book* (Moffat, Yard & Company, 1907), 29.

4   Patrick Lencioni, *The Five Dysfunctions of a Team: A Leadership Fable* (Jossey-Bass, 2002), 22.

5   J. Lachaud, A. A. Yusuf, F. Maelzer, et al., "Social Isolation and Loneliness Among People Living with Experience of Homelessness: A Scoping Review", *BMC Public Health* 24, 2515 (2024), https://doi.org/10.1186/s12889-024-19850-7.

6   Jim Collins, *Good to Great: Why Some Companies Make the Leap…and Others Don't* (HarperBusiness, 2001), 35–36.

7   Craig Groeschel, "How to Be Real and Not Be Weird," Life.Church, accessed April 14, 2026, https://www.life.church/leadershippodcast/how-to-be-real-and-not-be-weird/.

8   Paul Harvey was a popular radio broadcaster whose program *The Rest of the Story* aired from 1951 to 2008, reaching more than twenty-four million people per week. These stories were the little-known or iconic facts about people and events.

During one of my summer internships, my college dairy judging coach encouraged me to listen to Paul every day. He did this to help me learn how to use emphasis and dramatic pauses for effect, like Paul. This style made him a masterful storyteller and held tremendous audience attention. Several times in the last few years that I have been public speaking, people have come to me afterward, noting my dramatic pauses. I don't even know I do it now. I just spent an entire summer listening to an expert.

9   "O Holy Night" Presbyterian Church of Jackson Hole, December 13, 2022, https://pcjh.org/o-holy-night/.

10 Claude Silver, *Be Yourself at Work: The Groundbreaking Power of Showing Up, Standing Out, and Leading from the Heart* (HarperCollins, 2025), 33.

11 Jon Lewis, "NBA Finals Ratings History (1988–Present)," Sports Media Watch, accessed April 14, 2026, sportsmediawatch.com/nba-finals-ratings-viewership-history.

12 Sean Burch, "Why the NBA's Ratings Are Down Big," Yahoo Sports, December 2, 2024, https://sports.yahoo.com/why-nba-ratings-down-big-141500434.html.

13 Colin Salao, "NBA Ratings Are Dipping and One NBA Legend Has a Theory Why," Front Office Sports, November 8, 2024, https://frontofficesports.com/nba-ratings-are-dipping-and-one-nba-legend-has-a-theory-why/.

14 Jim Harter, "Anemic Employee Engagement Points to Leadership Challenges," Gallup, August 6, 2025, https://www.gallup.com/workplace/692954/anemic-employee-engagement-points-leadership-challenges.aspx.

15 Abraham Maslow, *The Psychology of Science: A Reconnaissance* (Harper & Row, 1966) 15–16.

16 Don't let the facts get in the way of a good story (Adapted from Frank Lewis Dyer and Thomas Commerford Martin,

Edison: His Life and Inventions [Harper & Brothers, 1910], and popular accounts of the Edison "letter story.")

17 Tyler Dickerhoof, host. 2021. The Tyler Dickerhoof Show, episode 9, "How to Clean Up Your Mental Mess with Dr. Caroline Leaf," March 12, https://podcasts.apple.com/us/podcast/ep-9-how-to-clean-up-your-mental-mess-with-dr-caroline-leaf/id1545349296?i=1000512664873.

18 Carol S. Dweck, *Mindset: The New Psychology of Success* (Random House, 2006), 7.

19 I've tried to find a softer, more socially acceptable term, but nothing fits. "Selfish" was suggested, but I don't think that covers the true essence. In the words of my AI partner, "The Empathy Spectrum hits harder because it names what leaders actually think but rarely say— that's what makes it memorable and real." Touché, my friend. Touché!

20 John C. Maxwell (@JohnCMaxwellOfficial), "Success is when I add value to myself, but significance is when I add value to others." Facebook, February 16, 2025, https://www.facebook.com/JohnCMaxwellOfficial/photos/success-is-when-i-add-value-to-myself-but-significance-is-when-i-add-value-to-ot/616934601069035/.

21 Michael Hyatt, *The Vision Driven Leader: 10 Questions to Focus Your Efforts, Energize Your Team, and Scale Your Business* (Baker, 2020).

22 Will Guidara, *Unreasonable Hospitality: The Remarkable Power of Giving People More than They Expect* (Optimism Press, 2022).

23 Michael Hyatt, The Vision Scripter (Full Focus, 2022), 10.

24 Steve Balestrieri, "Wanna Become a US Navy SEAL? Good Luck with That," 1945, December 28, 2024, https://www.19fortyfive.com/2024/12/wanna-become-a-u-s-navy-seal-good-luck-with-that/.

25 John C. Maxwell, *Put Your Dream to the Test: 10 Questions to Help You See It and Seize It* (Thomas Nelson, 2009).

26 Collins, *Good to Great*, 86.

www.ingramcontent.com/pod-product-compliance
Lightning Source LLC
Chambersburg PA
CBHW021529150726
47990CB00006B/2161